PUFFIN BOO

THREE LIONESSES

ELLA TOONE

GEORGIA STANWAY

NIKITA PARRIS

WRITTEN WITH CHERYL RICKMAN

PUFFIN

PUFFIN BOOKS

UK | USA | Canada | Ireland | Australia
India | New Zealand | South Africa

Puffin Books is part of the Penguin Random House group of companies
whose addresses can be found at global.penguinrandomhouse.com.
www.penguin.co.uk www.puffin.co.uk www.ladybird.co.uk

Penguin
Random House
UK

First published 2023
001

Text design by Dynamo
Spot illustrations by Dynamo
Printed in Great Britain by Clays Ltd, Elcograf S.p.A

The authorized representative in the EEA is Penguin Random House
Ireland, Morrison Chambers, 32 Nassau Street, Dublin D02 YH68

A CIP catalogue record for this book is available from the British Library

ISBN: 978–0–241–65723–2

All correspondence to:
Puffin Books
Penguin Random House Children's
One Embassy Gardens, 8 Viaduct Gardens,
London SW11 7BW

MIX
Paper | Supporting
responsible forestry
FSC® C018179
www.fsc.org

Penguin Random House is committed to a
sustainable future for our business, our readers
and our planet. This book is made from Forest
Stewardship Council® certified paper.

CONTENTS

Introduction   **1**

Part One: She Trains   **15**

     Chapter One: This is Me!   17

     Chapter Two: Believe in You!   55

     Chapter Three: Self-Care is Health Care   105

Part Two: She Shoots   **151**

     Chapter Four: Squad Goals   153

     Chapter Five: Taking Aim At What Matters Most   201

     Chapter Six: The Power of Purpose   223

Part Three: She Scores   **249**

    Chapter Seven: Goal!   251

Part Four: She Goes Again   **279**

    Chapter Eight: Bounce Back
    and Rise to Challenges   281

Extra Time   **331**

Useful Resources   **337**

To all those bold Lionesses who paved the way for us, and to the young Lionesses out there who will follow in our footsteps.

We dedicate this book to all of you.

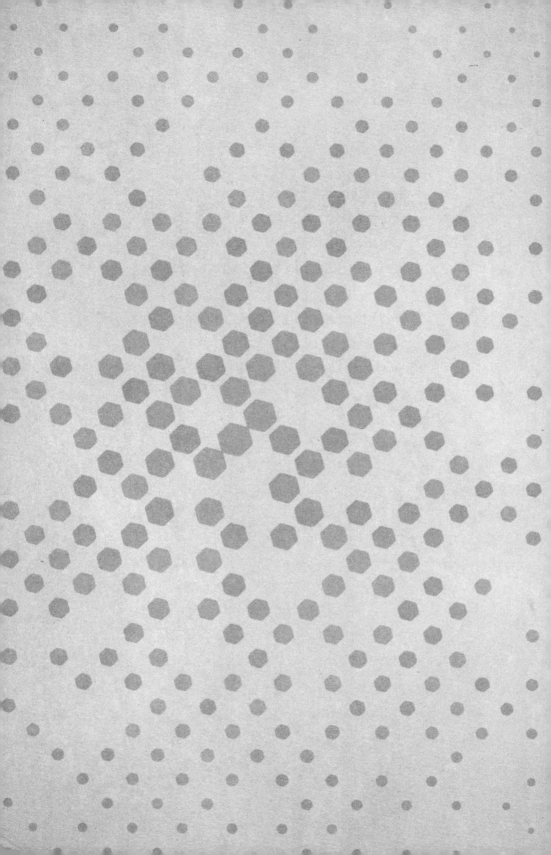

INTRODUCTION

HEY! We are Ella Toone (Tooney), Nikita Parris (Keets) and Georgia Stanway (G). We're all professional footballers. Tooney and Keets play for Manchester United, and G plays for Bayern Munich. You might know us if you watched the Women's European Championship during the summer of 2022 as we were all part of the England squad. This means we are Lionesses. And so are you.

You already have the spirit of the Lioness inside you – we all do! This book aims to bring that out of you, helping you find, build and embrace your inner Lioness.

In this book, we're going to talk to you about how to grow your confidence, find your team, learn from every win and loss in life, and work towards your goals. We'll share with you how we achieved our dreams, but we'll also reveal some of the mistakes we made along the way, what we learned from them, and how we've got back up when we've been knocked down (not just on the pitch!).

Nikita's going to share what she's learned about being yourself and finding your purpose, Ella's going to talk about doing what you love and finding balance, and Georgia's going to share her own Lioness lessons about the importance of self-care, why your responses matter and how everything (even the tough stuff) counts when it comes to living your best life.

Let's start with a question . . . Have you noticed that on every England football shirt there are three lions sitting proudly in a crest? And have you ever wondered why lions have been chosen as the country's symbol? Well, this symbol dates back more than 800 years to the year 1189, when Richard the Lionheart was the king of England. He had three lions on his shield, and this image became so popular that it was copied by other royals for hundreds of years – until eventually, the Football Association (the FA) chose the lions to feature on the country's kit!

CONFESSION: We didn't know any of this (none of us were particularly good at history at school!). To be honest, we didn't even know that the three lions have featured on the shirt of the national football team for over 150 years! That might be an embarrassing thing to admit, as all three of us have played for England, but there are going to be more confessions throughout this book. We want to be completely truthful and real with you about our own experiences, even the embarrassing or uncomfortable bits.

Symbols aside, one thing we *do* know is how proud each of us is every time we get to wear three lions on our shirts and represent our country. We were thrilled to find out that over fifty million people tuned in to watch us win the European Championships with the rest of our teammates in the summer of 2022.

That was a real high point – lifting that trophy up alongside our best friends – but it hasn't been an easy journey for any of us. We've worked *really* hard, we've had disappointments and setbacks to deal with, and we've had the extra challenge of trying to succeed in a sport that has typically been dominated by boys and men. But here we are – European champions – and we want to share our entire journey with you, and hopefully inspire you to go after your goals and be the best at whatever you put your mind to.

WE WANT YOU TO KNOW THAT YOU ARE AMAZING, AND WITH HARD WORK, DETERMINATION, CONFIDENCE AND RESILIENCE, YOU CAN REACH FOR YOUR DREAMS JUST LIKE WE DID!

YOU POWER!

It's easy to think that you have to be the best at something to be amazing – but that's not true. You are already brilliant because you're unique. There's nobody else like you on the planet!

Even if you're a twin (like Nikita), you are still unique. (For example, Nikita is a fussy eater, whereas her twin sister, Kelsey, will try *any* food.) Just like your fingerprint is unique to you and different from any of the other eight billion people on the planet, so are your individual strengths and weaknesses, personality traits, skills and dreams – and THAT individuality and uniqueness makes you amazing.

In this book, you're going to find out some stuff about us that you probably didn't already know. Like how Georgia's bad habit is biting her nails; or how Nikita was an altar girl from the age of nine, which means she used to help out the priest at church; or how Ella fainted on her first England training camp after the squad had blood tests done, and she woke up to find her best mate and teammate Abbie McManus filming her!

You're going to find out how we've dealt with the downs as well as the ups on the roller coaster of life. Because that is what life can be like, can't it? Things can be going well one minute, and then an obstacle gets in your way and you have to rise to the challenge. We'll also be here to remind you that even when things aren't going well, it doesn't last forever. Something good will be just around the corner, ready to lift you up and make you smile.

We want to help you navigate this roller-coaster ride. We're going to show you how to respond to the tough stuff and make the most of the good stuff, so you can cope with the twists and turns along the way. So, across these pages we'll give you some Lionesses' lessons to help you with that. (Keep an eye out for Tooney's Top Tips, Georgia's Great Guides and Nikita's Nifty Notes!)

Lionesses are courageous, they work in prides (teams), and they roar to make their voices heard. There's so much we can learn from them. We all have a Lioness inside and we want to help you embrace this to become your boldest and bravest self!

YOUR KITBAG

Footballers don't just turn up with a kit for each match. They need a whole kitbag, with shin pads, football boots, a water bottle and more inside.

But it's not just these physical objects that you need to carry in your bag to succeed. You also need a range of skills, a variety of character strengths (like grit, determination and resilience), and it also helps if you have supportive people in there too. (Yes, we realize that's quite a lot to put in a bag, but let's try and use our imaginations here!)

Now, we want you to imagine you have a kitbag in which you keep everything you need to succeed in your life. Across these pages, we're going to help you find the things you want to fill your imaginary bag with – your teammates, your strengths, your skills, your goals and more. And we're going to share with you some handy tools and team tactics that you can store in there too.

THE SIX PILLARS OF WELLBEING

The six pillars of wellbeing are six very important things to carry in your kitbag, in order to help you feel good, calm, confident and to thrive. According to wellbeing experts, if we regularly do stuff that builds on these six foundations, the happier we will be and the better we will function, both mentally and physically.

These six pillars are:

1. **POSITIVE EMOTION**
2. **ENGAGEMENT**
3. **RELATIONSHIPS**
4. **MEANING**
5. **ACCOMPLISHMENT**
6. **VITALITY**

Throughout this book, we are going to cover all of these six pillars in more detail – what they mean and how to build on them – so that you can pack them away in your kitbag and thrive in whatever you choose to do in life.

We love that playing football ticks all six boxes:

★ It makes us feel loads of different **POSITIVE EMOTIONS**, like gratitude, joy, hope, pride, interest, inspiration and awe. (I mean, did you see that back-heel goal from Alessia Russo vs Sweden in the Euros?! Now that was AWEsome!)

★ Football is an **ENGAGING** activity and the tight-knit teams give us the supportive **RELATIONSHIPS** we need.

★ Playing at the top of our game gives us the opportunity to create **MEANING**, because each of us is pursuing our goal and purpose.

★ Plus, each time we step on to the pitch we get the chance to **ACCOMPLISH** a new goal and reach a new target, which always feels good.

★ And as for **VITALITY**, the physicality of football means we are always as strong, active and energized as we can possibly be.

Think about what your imaginary kitbag looks like on the outside – you could even grab a pen and paper and draw it to help you visualize it. Ella's has her trainers tied to the handle by the laces; Nikita's kitbag is customized to look like a speaker because she loves music; and Georgia's, well, hers has her treasured Alan Shearer Match Attax football card from 2006 stuck on!

What would you customize your kitbag with? Think about all the things you love and you can cover your imaginary kitbag with stickers or pictures of those things.

GIRL POWER

OK, so your bag is packed, your laces are tied and you're almost ready to get started. But first, we have just one last reminder of why we want you to embrace your inner Lioness . . .

Remember we said we were a bit rubbish at history at school? Well, there are some parts of history that we do know about – like the fact that women were actually banned from playing football on Football League grounds for fifty years, from 1921 until 1971. The FA claimed that 'the game of football is quite unsuitable for females and ought not to be encouraged'. How unacceptable is that?! And women weren't even allowed to vote before 1918. Thankfully, women's rights (and women's football) have come a long way since then, but there's still a lot to be done.

Something us Lionesses did after winning the Euros (it still feels so good to write that . . .) was write an open letter to our then prime minister, Liz Truss, and the chancellor at the time, Rishi Sunak, demanding that young girls are given the opportunity to play football. We'd learned that only 63% of girls had the opportunity to play football in PE at school (in contrast to 100% of boys) and, because we believe the next generation – YOUR generation – deserve more, we wanted to use our voices and our platform to do something about it.

Whether you like playing football or not, we don't want you to feel held back in any way. Sometimes it feels like there are so many rules in society about what girls should look like, feel like and be like from an early age. We have heard them all, from 'you should get a proper job' to 'it's unladylike to run up and down a pitch all day'. These outdated and oversimplified ideas are called 'stereotypes'. We want you to smash through

GIRLS DESERVE TO HAVE THE CHOICE TO PLAY FOOTBALL AND DESERVE TO BELIEVE THAT THEY CAN ONE DAY PLAY FOR ENGLAND.

those old-fashioned, limiting stereotypes that say, 'this game or activity or colour' is for 'boys only' or 'girls only'.

We want you to JUST BE YOU – and that means being all that you are.

Keep doing the things you love and are good at, and practise doing the things you want to become better at. Don't let anything get in your way, and rise to whatever challenges come up, because we know you can do it. Accept the things you can't change about yourself – those unique parts of you that are just the way you are, whether that's being a bit clumsy, forgetful or too-this or not-enough-that. There's no such thing as 'too you', so celebrate all that you are. Because we believe in YOU!

ARE YOU READY TO EMBRACE YOUR INNER LIONESS?

Love from *Tooney, Keets and G* x

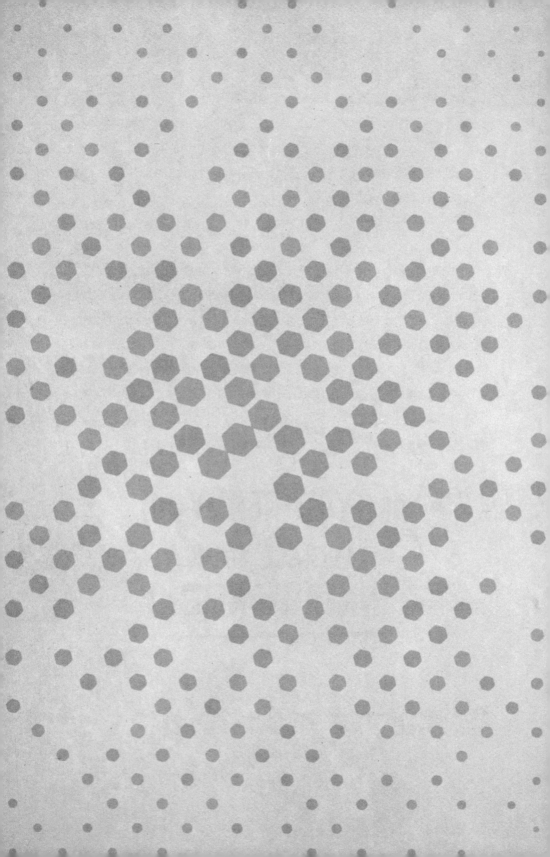

PART ONE
SHE TRAINS

CHAPTER ONE:
THIS IS ME!

NIKITA

'Girls don't play football!'
'Girls play with dolls, not footballs, Nikita!'
'Football isn't a female sport.'

These were the kinds of things I heard growing up. From my family, from friends, at school. But I didn't play with dolls. I played football. And I'm a girl. So, I was having none of it. I refused to be told what I should or shouldn't do based on my gender.

For me, football just felt right. It felt natural. But I'd always find myself hearing the same thing over and over again and having the same argument. I'd reply, tying my laces and grabbing a ball:

YOU'RE WRONG. GIRLS CAN PLAY FOOTBALL TOO!

It was so frustrating, but the funny thing was, these arguments just made me want to go and kick a ball! So I did!

Of course, it wasn't their fault they said those things. Apart from the fact it was boring for them (I'd always make them be goalkeeper so I could practise kicking balls at them), a lot of the girls around me *did* prefer playing with dolls to football. And that's OK too. That was their truth. That's what felt authentic to them.

THE SHOELACES OF SHOULD

The idea that girls should or shouldn't do certain things is told to us over and over again, by society, by our culture, by the media, by TV adverts, by the shopping aisles lined with pink clothes for girls and superhero toys for boys. We are told what we *should* play with, what we *should* look like and how we *should* dress from an early age, based on our gender. Then, as we get older, those 'shoulds' tell us what shape we *should* be, what we *should* do for a job, and so on. And if you're told something enough times repeatedly, you start to believe it.

But these 'shoulds' don't take into consideration that we're all individuals, who come in different shapes and sizes and have different interests.

For example, girls are often told they should be 'gentle' and 'sweet'. And sometimes girls who show strength and confidence and opinions are labelled as 'bossy'. These girls could go on to become brilliant leaders, but might feel held back if they're being criticized and labelled as bossy! Then if a boy shows the same traits, he is often labelled as a great leader, which would boost his confidence rather than making him doubt himself.

But these stereotypes can work against boys too. For example, boys are often told they should be tough and active, but this doesn't leave any room for gentle, thoughtful boys who prefer reading or writing to running around or playing sport.

Some girls don't realize how strong they are or how capable they are, because of these stereotypical 'shoulds'. And some boys struggle with expressing emotions because they're told that 'boys don't cry' or that they should 'man up'. Sometimes these 'shoulds' can make people feel ashamed or like they are 'wrong' in some way because they don't fit the stereotype, so they stop playing with cars or dolls or footballs – or whatever it is that they truly enjoy.

WE DON'T ALL FIT THE MOULD, BECAUSE WE'RE ALL UNIQUE INDIVIDUALS WITH A WIDE RANGE OF DIFFERENCES.

YOU'RE NEVER WRONG IF YOU ARE BEING TRUE TO YOU

I knew I *could* play football and I also knew that I shouldn't stop playing just because I was a girl. It's like saying you can't play football because you've got blonde hair, or you can't be a footballer because you're left-handed (or left-footed).

Imagine having the shoelaces from your left and right football boots tied together while you're wearing them. This would stop you from being able to run as freely as you want to. For me, the same can be said about these outdated 'shoulds'! They limit you and prevent you from going out into the world as your whole self. And it's only when you are free to be your whole self that you can give all that you have to offer.

I remember reading a book by singer, songwriter and global superstar Alicia Keys, called *More Myself*, where she said that the music industry expected women to be flawless. Because of this, she ended up dressing, speaking and behaving in a way that was a 'more digestible version' of herself. What she meant by this is that she had to change the way she was, because those 'shoulds' told her that she wasn't good enough, or that she wasn't the 'right' kind of woman. Can you believe it?! Alicia Keys, one of the most amazing, talented singer-songwriters of all time, being made to feel like she wasn't good enough.

But I want you to know that there's no such thing as 'too' this or 'not enough' that if you are being 100% you. Thankfully, Alicia realized this and chose to stop masking her whole self and just be all that she is. It made her more real, more relatable and it made her happier too. Doesn't that sound great?

Can you think of anything you hide or cover up about yourself because you are worried about what other people might think? Whether that's a hobby or interest that you haven't told anyone about, or a way of dressing and expressing yourself? Or maybe you don't try your hardest at school, because you think people might make fun of you?

I know you just want other people to like you and accept you. We all want that – it's human nature. But would you rather people like the true and whole you, or a version of you that has a part missing? The real you is more relatable than a masked you. And I guarantee you'll feel happier being the full, awesome version of you, rather than trying to hide it.

FIT IN OR BELONG

A feeling of belonging is a human need. As cave people living in prehistoric times, our ancestors couldn't survive on their own. They needed to hunt for food together and so it became part of human nature to need to be accepted by others. If we weren't deemed good enough, it could mean rejection from the group. That's why social approval matters so much to us humans. Belonging is a survival instinct – we're wired to feel that need strongly.

BUT THERE'S A BIG DIFFERENCE BETWEEN 'FITTING IN' AND 'BELONGING'.

Trying to 'fit in' means diluting or changing your true self to fit someone else's standards. It means following the herd instead of following your heart.

But 'belonging' means being who you really are, imperfectly, without changing, without trading in your true self – and being totally accepted as you are.

In order to get that sense of belonging, you have to be real – you have to be 100% YOU! You'll never truly belong if you are trying to be someone else. You can't fake it forever, as the real you will always come out at some point. And it's exhausting trying to be someone you're not. If you are truly yourself and accept all that you are, you will find people, *your* people, who make you feel like you belong.

Not everyone will like you. You won't be everybody's cup of tea, but that's OK! That'll help you get closer to finding the people whose cup of tea you are – the people you feel most at home with.

> **SO DON'T FOLLOW THE CROWD. BE YOURSELF. BECAUSE THAT CROWD MIGHT NOT BE GOING WHERE YOU WANT TO GO.**

MADE IN TOXTETH

The first place I felt like I truly belonged and was free to be me was on the courts in Toxteth, in Liverpool. There, I wasn't being the person I was in front of my mum or in front of my nan or in front of my teachers or even schoolmates. I just went to the courts to be my true authentic self and kick a ball around. This sense of belonging remained with each football team I've played for.

Although ten years apart, both my half-sister Tash and I felt different to other kids our age. Whenever we played, we were the only girls playing football with the boys. And when there were parties, we were the ones staying home to rest and prepare for the game while everyone else went out. We did things our own way to get where we wanted to be.

This mindset of self-acceptance and determination helped us both express ourselves freely and become the best versions of ourselves. It's paid off because, even when Tash became injured and had to stop her own football career early, she just kept going. And I'm proud to say, at the time of publication, my half-sister Natasha Jonas is the world boxing junior middleweight champion and I'm a European football champion! For me, this proves the value of refusing to be held back by limiting 'shoulds' and choosing to be your true self.

Do you have a place you can go where you feel like you belong? Or a hobby or interest that makes you feel your happiest? It could be at the theatre. Or at a dance class. Or in your local park. Or in the school playground with your friends. Or at home with your family. Perhaps it's when you're playing chess, or writing, or reading. Wherever or whatever it is, keep going! No matter what anyone tells you, you deserve to find the thing or place you love most, and to truly enjoy it!

After joining Everton's Centre of Excellence (the team's youth academy) at age fourteen, I gradually became good enough to get a call-up to an England Under-15s training camp in Loughborough. I'd never been away from home for two nights, so was already feeling nervous when a chauffeur-driven black BMW pulled up outside our house. I'd never been in a BMW, let alone one with a chauffeur . . .

'Is that just for me?' I asked. Turned out it was!

It also turned out that my mum had already decided what I'd be wearing. She's got a thing about everything matching so there I was, being driven to the England training camp wearing a pink tracksuit with pink socks, a pink hairband and everything pink!

Arriving at camp, I soon noticed that all the other girls were wearing their clubs' football kits. Not me – oh no! I stood out like a bright pink piece of tinsel. I was mortified. And it was so ironic. I was used to feeling different at home, among girls who didn't have the same interests as me and who didn't dress the same as me. But here was a group of girls who *were* the same as me – girls who loved football – a group I belonged to without changing who I was. And they were wearing what I usually wore, yet here I was, still looking different! If I'd just worn my usual outfit of a football kit or dark tracksuit, I wouldn't have stood out at all. Face palm . . .

DANCE TO YOUR OWN DRUMBEAT

There are two things that I believe helped me gain the confidence I needed to be the most *me* I could be:

★ my own self-acceptance.

★ being inspired by the strong women around me.

These two things gave me a real passion for doing what I loved, and encouraged me to always dance to the beat of my own drum.

I remember when my mum bought me a Barbie bike. 'You are a girl,' she said. 'You've got to have some girly things.'

My mum worked hard to make sure we had all we needed. She was a single parent who had three jobs to take care of us four kids, so I definitely didn't want to ask her for a

different bike. But I also wasn't going to let the fact that I didn't have a BMX bike like the boys stop me from riding on my neighbour's ramp and enjoying myself. I decided to style the Barbie bike up and put my own stamp on it — to customize it. I got rid of the stabilizers and the pink tassels on the back wheels and I threaded a drink carton through the back tyre to make it noisy whenever I cycled around!

Before long, I was zooming up and down the ramp on this tiny pink bike alongside the boys' BMXs. My mum looked out of the window and laughed. After a while, she realized that no matter what she did, I wasn't going to fit the girly stereotype. Mum gradually accepted this, and, in the end, she was proud of my individuality.

And it was that determination to never abandon my true self that started me on my way to becoming a Lioness.

DIFFERENT IS GOOD

My teachers used to say that 'the world would be a very boring place if we were all the same'.

That's true and the world needs difference. And it's not just about different interests or different fashion styles. The world needs people from different ethnicities and different backgrounds, whether that's at school, in youth clubs, in team sports, or, as you get older, in workplaces and companies. There are lots of studies that show the benefits of diversity.

For example, company workplaces, inclusive ones – with a mixture of people from different backgrounds, races, genders and sexualities – have been shown to come up with better ideas and perform better overall. This is because each person can offer fresh perspectives gained from their different experiences and bring their own ideas, skills and strengths to the long, shiny boardroom table. That melting pot of difference is what creates brilliance.

Imagine two teachers set a school project to come up with ideas for a brand-new sports brand. One teacher splits the class into groups of people who have very similar backgrounds and experiences to one another. The other teacher creates more diverse groups with people from different backgrounds, with different skills and a mixture of ethnicities and genders. The diverse groups would likely have a wider variety of ideas and spark more creative discussions, because they bring a wider range of perspectives and skills to the table.

It's the same with football teams. In the teams I've played for, we have plenty in common – we all love football, of course! – but we don't all have the same strengths. We each bring something different to the squad and we play in different positions – attack, defence, midfield. Our unique skills complement each other to make a winning team. And, off the pitch, we each have different personalities, characteristics, backgrounds and quirks too.

Tooney loves having long eyelashes and getting her nails painted, for example. Whereas Georgia and I have never really had much interest in these things. Georgia is an expert suitcase packer and is very good at keeping things tidy, whereas Ella prefers to just chuck stuff in a case and zip it up. That's the point – there's no one way to be human, and the world is a much more interesting, open and kinder place when we learn to embrace and welcome each other's differences and allow people to be themselves.

NIKITA'S NIFTY NOTES ON BEING YOUR TRUE SELF

★ Instead of questioning whether you're good enough, ask yourself, are you being YOU enough?

★ Another person's opinion can only affect you if you allow it. When you realize that you're never going to please everyone, you can be free.

★ Like that Barbie bike, customize yourself to suit your individuality. Behave, dress and speak according to your true self. You are enough as you are. Never compromise yourself for the approval of others.

★ Appreciate other people's differences as well as your own.

★ You do you.

ELLA

IMPERFECTLY PERFECT

I'm not a very good cook. I'm also very loud. My mum's always saying, 'Why are you shouting, Ella?' And I don't even realize I'm shouting. I'm just talking, but I just happen to talk really loudly.

Some might say being 'too loud' or 'not good at cooking' are my imperfections. And I'm happy to share them with you because nobody's perfect.

Have you ever been told you're 'too' this or 'not enough' that? And are there things that you're just not very good at? Well, you're not alone. No one is good at everything, but your imperfections are what make you *you*.

It's really important to accept your imperfections because you wouldn't be you without them. I wouldn't be me if I wasn't a bit loud. Keets wouldn't be her without her banter and if G didn't tell it like it is, she wouldn't be her.

‘AS LONG AS YOUR **IMPERFECTIONS AREN'T** HURTING ANYBODY, YOU SHOULDN'T HAVE TO CHANGE **FOR ANYONE.**’

Then there's the stuff you're not very good at, which you might want to get better at. But you don't have to improve *everything* you're bad at. It's all right for some weaknesses to stay as weaknesses. And, if you're still enjoying what you're doing, then just carry on. There's no need to be the best at everything!

Deciding what you want to improve and what you want to accept about yourself is massive. I mean, I know I *could* become better at cooking if I wanted to and practised (A LOT!), but I'm not going to be hard on myself for not having the time in my life right now to focus on improving that skill. (Keets, on the other hand, loves to cook, so I could always go round to hers for a nice meal, eh, Keets? What are we havin'?)

But if there are things that you care about – maybe there's a particular subject at school that you want to do better at, for example – there's nothing wrong with dedicating more of your energy to developing those skills.

Finding the right balance between self-improvement and self-acceptance is tricky, but we are here to help!

TOONEY'S TOP TIPS ON BALANCING ACCEPTANCE WITH IMPROVEMENT

★ Identify your imperfections and the things you find difficult.

★ Work out which of these things aren't hurting anyone and aren't impacting your own life in a bad way – can you learn to accept these flaws?

★ Don't be hard on yourself for not being the best at everything.

★ Focus on just one or two things to improve and devote time and energy towards that. If you try to do too much, you'll be too exhausted to get better at anything at all!

★ Be proud of yourself for focusing on self-improvement, while also accepting that nobody is perfect.

★ Self-acceptance isn't just an excuse to give up on something you struggle with. It's always worth having a go at improving something, even if it's hard.

AN ATTITUDE OF GRATITUDE

I've learned that this whole 'balance' thing is a massive part of living a good and happy life – like balancing work and play, comfort and adventure, activity and chilling out in my joggers. You also need to balance taking care of others with self-care. And outdoor time with indoor time. And I need to try to balance pushing myself to improve with being grateful for what I've already got.

As a professional footballer, I'm always focused on developing, growing and striving to be even better. So I think a lot about all I still want to achieve. Scoring a goal at Old Trafford would be the ultimate goal – the icing on the cake for me. But to balance that out, it's also important for me to spend time thinking about what I'm most grateful for right now and about what I've already done. I find it helpful to write this out in a list.

THINGS I'M GRATEFUL FOR:

★ I'm massively grateful for everything I've achieved so far in my career: from scoring on my debut in the Senior England squad, to scoring a goal at Wembley in the Euros final and becoming a European champion sixteen months later, to being the record goal scorer for Manchester United – the team I supported growing up.

★ I'm grateful that I get paid to play football with my friends.

★ Most of all, I'm grateful for my family. I wouldn't have achieved any of that success without them and the sacrifices they've made over the years: the amount of times they drove me to training and back; the fact that they've been to every single game to watch me, home and away, whether in England or abroad. They've been there supporting me through it all, celebrating the good times and picking me up during the harder bits.

YOUR **TURN**

Do you have a notepad that you could turn into your gratitude journal? Use it to write down what you're grateful for. You can write what you appreciate about yourself, who you're grateful to have in your life, anything at all.

And you can do this every day – spend some time in the evening writing down three good things you're grateful for that happened during the day.

It can be fun to read back through your notes later. That's the good thing about recording gratitude – it makes you feel good over and over again (when you first write it down and then whenever you read it back!).

Even on difficult days, when you might struggle to find something that's gone well, you will find that there is always *something* to be grateful for, even if it's something quite small – a smile from a friend, a peaceful moment with a pet, a hug from a relative.

FOCUSING ON THE POSITIVES

Have you ever found yourself thinking about that one negative mark you received, even though you often get pretty good marks for most of your work? Or dwelling on the one mean comment someone made to you, when most people were probably being nice? Or the one thing you've done badly instead of all the things you did well?

Me too! It's weird, because when I post something online on my social media, there could be hundreds of nice comments full of love and praise, but I always remember the one little negative comment that someone makes.

I used to do this on the pitch as well. No matter how well I'd played throughout the match, if I gave the ball away to the other team on just one occasion, I'd end up focusing on that, telling myself I'm a terrible player. I'd tune in to that one bad move instead of all the good ones – focusing on the negatives and not the positives.

Being able to train your brain to think more about the positive things, or to focus on what you're doing right or what you can do next, is massive and can have amazing consequences. And I've had a great teacher who's helped me learn that and put it into practice. Can you guess who that teacher might be?

It's Sarina Wiegman – manager and head coach of England's national women's football team.

During one game, I was brought off at half-time. Sarina said to me, 'You need to stop being so hard on yourself, because that's when you don't play well. It's because you're thinking about a mistake you've made and focusing on that instead of focusing on the next thing.'

I just remember thinking, 'I never want to be brought off at half-time ever again.' So, I needed to sort it out; to change my attitude and shift my mindset to find the good.

In that moment, I realized it's OK to make mistakes. It doesn't mean I'm a bad footballer, it just means I'm trying things out, being brave and taking risks. And sometimes the risk doesn't pay off. And that's OK.

UNREALISTIC EXPECTATIONS

Throughout my life, I have always wanted to be the best I can be. But at times this has turned into perfectionism – where I want to be PERFECT at everything. This is unrealistic. No one can ever get EVERYTHING right ALL of the time, and striving for this can make losing or failing or making mistakes harder to accept.

There's nothing wrong with wanting to win and improve and be the best you can be. It shows you care, it shows you're driven and passionate about what you do. And if I didn't care about winning and hadn't pushed myself to keep improving, I wouldn't have got to where I am today. But, you can't expect to win every time and be the best at everything. And if you beat yourself up over every single mistake, having set yourself unrealistic expectations, you'll only end up making more mistakes, because your head isn't in the right place.

These days I still expect a lot from myself and have high standards because I know what I'm capable of and I believe in myself. I just know now to stay calm and stay in control of my mind. That's important in football because things can change in an instant.

I remember once when we played West Ham, I came on and assisted the equalizer.

'Yes, Tooney!' the crowd roared.

But about two minutes later, there was a tackle on the edge of our box. I gave away a free kick, and West Ham scored and won. I'd just gone from hero to zero in a few minutes.

I suppose the up-and-down nature of a football match is much like an exaggerated version of normal life. Like, one day you might feel on top of the world, like a superhero, then the next day, things might go wrong and get you down. But like Sarina showed me – you have a choice. You can stay stuck on zero and let it affect you, or you can shake it off, learn your lessons and be a hero again tomorrow.

The expectation to be perfect and never mess up is unrealistic. But there's a difference between trying hard to do your best, which is doable, and expecting perfection every time, which isn't.

'YOU CAN'T GET EVERYTHING RIGHT, EVERY MATCH, EVERY DAY. NOBODY CAN.'

Now I react better on the pitch and, when I do inevitably make a mistake, I've learned a better reaction is to ask myself, 'What can I do now?' Whether that's win the ball back straight away or defend, instead of dwelling on it. Now I replace 'Oh no! What have I done?' with 'OK, that just happened! What next?'.

Of course, I'm only human, so if I mess up, I still get annoyed with myself for a moment, because I know I'm capable of better. But I've got much better at not being so hard on myself that it affects my game.

BUT I DON'T WANT TO BE EATEN . . .

As we've now discovered, our brains are like sticky chewing gum for negative stuff, and like non-stick saucepans for the positive. And just as it's much harder to shake those thoughts about what we've done wrong than what we've done right, the same goes for those thoughts where we're worried about what *could* go wrong instead of what *might* go well.

For so long I thought it was just me who was like this! But worrying or judging ourselves harshly is part of being a normal human being. It turns out there's a good reason why we have this 'negativity bias'. And it's because of those cave people again!

Back in the Stone Age, when danger lurked round every corner, we needed to be on high alert in case a massive sabre-tooth tiger jumped out at us. And we needed to give ourselves a hard time when we made a mistake, because the stakes were high. One mistake could mean life or death for your whole family! So, focusing on the negatives was just a survival mechanism. It was much better to think about what could possibly go wrong so you could stop it from happening. If you just walked around thinking 'nah, it'll be fine' . . . you would probably get eaten!

So, back in the day, thinking about the worst-possible-case scenario was useful. Annoyingly, nobody has told our brains that we don't face the same level of danger as we did back then. So our brains are still wired to remember the mistakes and focus on the negatives.

This is why it's massively important to focus on balancing out negative thoughts with positivity.

Sometimes the positives are easy to find, like when you nail something you've been trying to do for ages, or when your mate has been making you laugh all day. Other times, you probably have to look harder for little moments of positivity. So, what can we do to tackle that negative-biased brain of ours?

FIND THE GOOD

You've already written in a gratitude journal. You can also try making a 'list of delights'! A friend of mine writes down little notes about what delights her, like the smell of chocolate cake in the oven or putting on warm socks fresh from the radiator. On mine I'd put 'getting home and tea being on the table' (especially if it's steak, egg and chips, or lasagne – cooked by my boyfriend, of course . . . because I still can't cook!).

It's your turn again! What would you include on your list of delights? Grab a pen and paper and start making that list now. Hopefully, it will be as long as your body, if you list down everything that makes you smile! Next time your mind starts wandering to negative thoughts and you can't seem to stop it, whip out this list. Remind yourself of the things that bring you joy and see if you can surround yourself with these things to lift your mood.

Another way to shift your mind towards positivity is to use photos. I really enjoy looking through my camera roll, my social media posts or photo albums from years ago to encourage my brain to focus on the good stuff.

Looking back at happy events is a great way to make the most of each positive moment. You get to feel good about them not once, not twice, but three times. First when you're looking forward to something, second while you're there enjoying the moment as it happens, then again when you look back and reminisce. It's mad because looking at a picture brings so many happy memories flooding back that you might have forgotten all about.

This can be a good way to turn the volume down on something negative for a bit and turn the volume up on happy memories and good things. That's not to say you should ignore or push away sad or angry or frustrated feelings. It's important for your mental health to express those feelings (by writing them down, talking about them to someone you trust, exercising to release that energy, or even having a good cry), but looking back at anything good can be a good way to soothe that negativity and find your balance.

What photographs make you smile? Can you keep copies of them somewhere close to you, somewhere you're able to access them easily whenever you need to?

THE POWER OF POSITIVITY

Positivity is a powerful tool to keep in your kitbag. Scientists have found that the better we feel, the better we do at everything in life – whether that's football, school, homework, remembering lines for a play or being a decent friend.

Feeling good also helps us think clearly. It's harder to focus when we're worried and anxious or beating ourselves up about something we've done wrong. (That's why Sarina pulled me off at half-time – giving myself a hard time would cloud my judgement.) So, it makes sense to look for the good at every opportunity – sort of like a joy detective – in order to do your best and be your best self!

SELF-ACCEPTANCE

Finding the good in yourself, accepting and owning who you are and learning to *love* who you are is so important.

For me, there was a turning point where I just thought, 'This is me. This is who I am. And I'm not going to change for anyone, so I might as well just get on with being me and love being me while I'm at it.' And do you know what? As soon as I did that, I realized that other people love me for being me as well, so why would I ever change that?

'THE MORE YOU ACCEPT, OWN AND LOVE ALL THAT YOU ARE, THE EASIER IT IS TO BELIEVE IN YOURSELF WITH THE BRAVERY AND CONFIDENCE OF A LIONESS.'

Georgia, Nikita and I really want you to love who you are too. Even the parts of you that you might have wished you could change, before you realized you wouldn't be your true self without them. Always remember that there is only one YOU in the world and that's your power.

CHAPTER TWO: BELIEVE IN YOU!

ELLA

It all started in 2004, when I was just five years old. Mrs Rushforth walked into the William Hill bookie's (a betting shop) in Tyldesley, a town in Manchester. 'I'd like to place a bet, please,' she said. 'Fifty pounds on my granddaughter Ella Toone to play for the England football team one day.' The odds were 1,000–1 (which means they believed it was *very* unlikely to happen), and they wouldn't let her pay more than £50 for the bet.

Jump forward sixteen years to a crisp September day in 2020. I was walking our dog, Norman, when my phone rang. I looked down at the screen and saw that Phil Neville, the England manager at the time, was calling me. I'd spoken to him a couple of times before about how I was getting on; I'd scored a decent amount of goals for Manchester United the previous season and had represented the country at youth level since playing in the 2016 FIFA U-17 Women's World Cup in Jordan, but I wasn't expecting this call.

'You're coming to my next camp,' announced Phil.

I was shocked into silence for a minute. 'Um. Thank you!' I finally replied, completely gobsmacked that I'd actually been called up for my first senior England camp. My inability to speak meant the phone call was a short one!

I rang my dad straight away. He was buzzing for me. He told me that I deserved it, that I'd been playing well and to just go and smash it. Then he got straight on the phone to my mum, and she was buzzing too.

And then it was time to call my nan.

'Hello, Nan, it's Ella!' I shouted down the phone (she's a bit hard of hearing, is my nan). 'I'm going to my first England camp,' I told her. I had to repeat myself a few times before she heard what I said. But when she eventually realized what I was telling her, she was over the moon!

My nan has been my biggest fan since I was really little. 'Well,' she said, 'that's why I put the bet on in the first place. I knew you'd do it!'

And my nan's belief in me paid off. Sixteen years later, when I was selected for the England team, she got £1,050 back from the bet she'd placed all those years ago. With the winnings, my nan gave £1,000 to me, and split the remaining £50 between my brother and cousin (she couldn't let them go without!).

My whole family have always supported my football. My nan's always at my home games and my dad hasn't

missed a game – not a single one. This has spurred me on whenever I've doubted myself. My family's belief in me has helped so much throughout my career, and has encouraged me to believe in myself. And that's important, because sometimes, especially when you're young, having that belief in yourself can be hard.

Self-belief is powerful in all sport, and without self-belief, I don't know if I'd have been able to get to where I am today. That's one of the reasons this book matters so much to me. Because I know how important it is to build up your own self-belief. I want to be able to help you do that, whether you have a bunch of believers around you or not. I believe in you. In fact, all three of us do.

"WE WANT TO TEACH YOU HOW TO BACK YOURSELF, BECAUSE YOU ARE DEFINITELY WORTH BACKING!"

Keets, G and I have been very lucky because, as well as our families, we have the support from our teams' fans cheering us on and filling us with confidence. But what if you don't (or it feels like you don't) have any cheerleaders around you, rooting for you and cheering you on? What do you do then?

WELL, TWO THINGS I RECKON TO BE TRUE ARE:

1. You will find your own cheerleaders in time. It only takes one person to believe in you to make a difference to how you feel about yourself. (We'll talk more about finding your team in chapter four.)

2. You can't just rely on others to believe in you. Whether you have a hundred supporters, one or none, you still need to become your own cheerleader. The people who believe in you won't always be there by your side in every moment, so it's important that you also believe in yourself. And you need to back yourself when it feels like nobody else is.

WHAT IS SELF-BELIEF?

Believing in yourself doesn't mean that you think you're better than everyone else. Not at all! Self-belief just means you can see what you bring to the world, to your family, to your friendships and to your own life. It means you can see your value, your strengths and your skills. And it means you know that you have what it takes to learn, improve and achieve your goals.

Obviously, even the most confident person will doubt themselves sometimes and feel like they're not good enough. We're only human, aren't we? But the good news is it's possible for everyone to build their self-belief. Remember . . .

★ Some things will come naturally to you and other things won't.

★ Sometimes you'll feel like you're terrible at EVERYTHING!

★ And sometimes you'll just feel a bit unsure of yourself. This is all normal!

But you can build your confidence step by step. Especially if you:

1. Are your true self, rather than trying to be someone you're not.

2. Try your best.

3. Practise, practise, practise!

4. Find and develop your superpowers.

5. Celebrate your wins.

We're going to be looking at all of these steps in this chapter, to help you become your own cheerleader!

COMPARE AND DESPAIR

Social media is a massive part of life now. There are hundreds of websites, apps and games that connect you to people online – whether that's with your next-door neighbour or friends who live on the other side of the world! You might not be on social media yet, or perhaps you have an account on every app out there, depending on your age – either way, I want to tell you the honest truth about how it can be both a good and bad thing for self-belief.

Social media can be a great way to express yourself online and communicate with friends and people you know. It can be a good place to learn and connect with others. But it can have a negative impact as well. When you're constantly looking at other people's social media, where they share and record all the good things about their lives, their clothes, their gadgets and their huge groups of friends, you can end up comparing yourself to others and feeling down. It's natural to compare yourself and your life to other people's sometimes, but doing this too much can really impact your mental health.

This is called 'compare and despair', and it doesn't just apply to social media. If you spend too long focusing on what other people are doing – whether that's on social media or even just in day-to-day life – you can end up feeling jealous, sad or like you're not good enough. And comparing yourself to someone else is pointless anyway. No one tends to share the worst or most embarrassing or shameful parts of their life, which means you end up comparing your *worst* bits to their *best* bits.

AND OFTEN SOME OF THOSE BEST BITS HAVE BEEN EDITED OR FILTERED TO MAKE THEM LOOK EVEN BETTER THAN THEY REALLY ARE. IT'S LIKE COMPARING YOUR 'BLOOPERS' REEL TO THEIR 'HIGHLIGHTS' REEL!

You really can never know someone else's full story. The person who has just been on holiday might have had a massive row with a sibling. The person with beautiful hair might be feeling self-conscious. The person with new clothes might be struggling in school. There's often more going on behind the screen and behind the scenes. And guess what? If the person you're comparing yourself with knew the real you, there's a good chance they'd want something you have and want to be more like you. (Trust me, you are probably much better than you think you are!)

So instead of comparing yourself to others and worrying about whether you're looking good enough, being funny enough and doing well enough by comparison, it makes much more sense to focus on trying your best and being as YOU as you can be, because that is always good enough.

❝ ONLY THEN CAN YOU LEARN TO LOVE YOURSELF FOR WHO YOU ARE, AND DEVELOP THE SELF-BELIEF YOU NEED TO GO AFTER YOUR DREAMS. ❞

BE INSPIRED

Sometimes it can feel intimidating when you see someone inspiring who has achieved everything you want to achieve in your own life. I've definitely felt this in the past with professional footballers I've met! But you can choose to let inspirational people lift you up rather than get you down. For example, when two World-Cup-winning players from the USA came to play at Manchester United, instead of comparing myself to them and letting myself feel inadequate, I looked to them for inspiration. I was like a sponge and soaked up as much as I could from them, asking questions and learning. Instead of 'compare and despair', I tried out 'compare and inspire'. And I discovered so much about them, and about myself too.

> SO, NEXT TIME YOU FIND YOURSELF COMPARING AND DESPAIRING, INSTEAD I WANT YOU TO ASK YOURSELF WHAT YOU CAN LEARN FROM THAT PERSON.

Think about the people in your life or those you see on TV who are doing what you want to do. Who can you learn from? Is it a world leader? A professional singer? A sports star? An author? A doctor? A teacher? Even a friend at school? Don't be intimidated by their success. Instead, allow them to spark some inspiration inside you and see how this can encourage you to go after your goals.

THE DREADED MEDIA INTERVIEW

Something you have to do as a professional footballer is media interviews. Urgh! I used to hate doing *anything* in front of the camera, and these interviews used to fill me with dread. It's weird because once you get to know me, I'm actually quite a confident person, but at first I can appear quite shy. It just takes me a little while to come out of my shell and feel comfortable.

Whenever I'd stand in front of a camera, I'd get the *sweatiest* palms. I would overthink everything and worry 'What if I say something wrong?' or 'What if I look silly?'. So, I would try to act all professional and serious-like . . . but that's not really me.

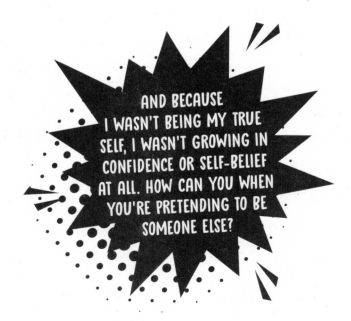

AND BECAUSE I WASN'T BEING MY TRUE SELF, I WASN'T GROWING IN CONFIDENCE OR SELF-BELIEF AT ALL. HOW CAN YOU WHEN YOU'RE PRETENDING TO BE SOMEONE ELSE?

Once, after winning the league with Manchester United, I did an interview after the game that went viral. It's funny now when I look back on it, but at the time I couldn't think about it without cringing! I was so nervous about messing up the interview that I ended up using a completely made-up word by mistake. I said that the match was 'memoriable' . . . Ha! What does that even mean?! It was probably because I was so worried about getting something wrong that I did it. I just panicked.

The problem was, I couldn't dread interviews forever, because one day I might score at Wembley and have to do an interview after the game!

" THE WOMEN'S GAME WAS GROWING MASSIVELY, SO I NEEDED TO GROW WITH IT TOO. "

As we covered in the last chapter, the first thing I knew I needed to do was accept my flaws. And I did! I accepted that I'm not perfect at giving interviews – and that's not my job anyway. My job is to kick a ball around the field, and interviews are just something that come with it.

Then once I'd accepted my imperfections, I needed to get rid of all that doubt in my head and realize what I *can* bring to an interview. I decided that I could use these interviews to get my personality across, to show who I really am – to show I'm just a normal fun-loving girl from Wigan who happens to be a footballer. And the more interviews I did, the more I got used to them.

Now I just take them in my stride. Most of the time I end up chatting a load of rubbish, but this is just who I am – a girly girl with an occasionally loud voice who loves football. And now I'm known for being a bit cheeky in front of the camera and just being myself – and that feels good!

Another way to build your self-belief is by trying your best.

I used to struggle with exams at school. My mum would always say 'just try your best'. And that's all you can ever do in life. If you try your very best, you can't be hard on yourself, because you know you couldn't have given any more. I take this mindset into training and games and everything else I do now.

Trying my best in football means giving 100% to make things happen for the team. It means working hard by putting the effort in, doing my job and making sure I go out on to the pitch, get on the ball, enjoy it and leave nothing behind.

Outside of football, something I try my best to do is be a good person, be a good friend and be there for the people who are always there for me.

What does trying your best look like for you? It could mean trying your best at school or in a subject or sport you enjoy, or trying to be the best sibling or friend you can be. Maybe being your best self is about trying to be helpful or kind whenever you get the chance? Have a think about what the best version of you is like. We're going to help you get there!

PRACTISE, PRACTISE, PRACTISE!

The way to be sure that you are trying your best is to practise, practise and practise some more. When I was little, I used to google 'Ronaldo skills' and then go out into the garden and practise them. The more I practised, the better I got, and that's the same with anything. Practice helps your muscles and your mind remember how to do something, as you repeat the action over and over again.

You might be thinking, 'Oh, it's all right for you, Ella, you're naturally talented at football.' But while it's true that some things come more naturally to me and other things might come more naturally to you, it's important to have what psychologists call a 'growth mindset'.

At the United Academy, where I went as a young girl, they used to say, 'Hard work beats talent when talent doesn't work hard.' This means you can be talented but, if you don't work hard, you won't get as far as someone who puts in the effort to practise.

A GROWTH MINDSET IS THE BELIEF THAT YOU CAN IMPROVE IN WHATEVER YOU DO AND GET BETTER OVER TIME BY PUTTING IN THE EFFORT. IT'S ALWAYS WORTH TRYING, BECAUSE YOU CAN IMPROVE MOST THINGS WITH PRACTICE, WHETHER SOMETHING COMES NATURALLY TO YOU OR NOT.

71

SEEING YOUR STRENGTHS

Remember in the chapter before this we talked about why accepting your imperfections is important? Well, it's also important to notice your strengths, so you can work on building and developing these. The more you do that, the more you'll believe in yourself and your (growing) capabilities.

> WHEN HUMANS LIVED IN CAVES, IMPROVING OUR WEAKNESSES WAS KEY TO HELPING US SURVIVE. BUT NOW WE KNOW THAT FOCUSING ON OUR STRENGTHS IS WHAT HELPS US TO THRIVE.

When it comes to football, I know what I'm really good at (finding pockets of space, getting on the half-turn, making passes and driving with the ball). I know my energy levels and my ability to get around the pitch are good. I also know what I need to work on improving (using my body better and not being so hard on myself, for instance).

In day-to-day life, I also know and accept that I'm not very good at cooking, cleaning or dancing! But in regular life, it's not always easy to notice what we're *good* at. Sometimes, when something comes naturally to us, we might not notice it as a strength. Like, say you're a really good listener and you always seem to know what to say to make people feel better when they're feeling down – you might not see that as a strength because it's just what you do. But that's one of your superpowers and the more you notice and use your superpowers, the more you can grow in confidence and boost your belief in yourself.

TOONEY'S TOP TIPS ON FINDING YOUR SUPERPOWERS

STEP ONE

Think about three or four things that other people have said you do well, or that you think you're pretty good at, whether it's an activity or a personality trait. It could be anything, from listening to someone when they're down, making people laugh, sport, drawing or cooking – or anything else at all! (If you're struggling to think of any, go and ask someone close to you what they think your strengths are.)

STEP TWO

Now grab a pen and paper and write down your strengths.

STEP THREE

Next time you feel self-doubt or like you aren't good enough, come back to this list. Focus on your own individual unique strengths, and watch your self-belief grow!

STEP FOUR

Harness those superpowers, by using them, practising them, growing them and allowing yourself to become the best version of you.

WEAR YOUR STRENGTHS WITH PRIDE

Sometimes things will happen that boost your belief in yourself – it could be when a teacher gives you a good mark, or when a family member or coach or friend says something as simple as 'nice one'. People don't always have to shower you with praise to tell you that you're doing OK. It could be a smile, a nod or a pat on the back.

For me, it was the number 7 shirt.

When I was eighteen, I was invited to join Manchester United's first-ever women's team. Casey Stoney, the head coach who I'd been a massive fan of growing up, called us all in for a meeting and gave us each a box. I opened my box and noticed a shirt inside. But not just any shirt. A shirt with the number 7 on the back. In shock, I whispered, 'Is that my shirt?' Casey looked at me and smiled: 'Yeah, that's your number.'

The number 7 shirt is iconic at Manchester United. Every player who's worn the number 7 has been a legend, from Bryan Robson and Eric Cantona to David Beckham and Cristiano Ronaldo. Not only that, number 7 was on the back of every Manchester United shirt I wore growing up!

Casey knew how much the number 7 meant at the club, and she'd given it to me. Casey Stoney, an icon of women's football, believed in me. This gave me a lot more confidence and a massive boost of self-belief. It also gave me hope that I could inspire other young girls who might want to be the next number 7 at Manchester United.

So today, I want to gift you with a number 7 shirt.

OK, I can't gift you an actual shirt because this is just a book. I'm sorry! But I want you to trace this shirt on to a piece of paper. And above the 7, write your name. If you like, you can even write your superpowers round the number, to remind yourself of your own awesomeness.

Just like the number 7 shirt was such a boost for me, I hope this little shirt can be the same for you – a reminder that with confidence and self-belief, you too can go far.

CELEBRATE EVERY WIN

When Prince William put that European Championship medal round my neck after we won the Euros, it was a massive 'pinch me' moment. There I was, hugging the future king of England, who was beaming from ear to ear with pride. I was crying, then I was laughing. Then I was in shock about what we'd just done. In that moment I thought to myself:

❝ ELLA! WE'VE FINALLY DONE IT! WE'VE ACTUALLY BROUGHT FOOTBALL HOME! ❞

I could hear the crowd cheering, clapping and whistling. It was so loud in the stadium, and everyone was just buzzing. And to get to share that moment with some of my best friends made it even better. So did the fact that we were the first football team, male or female, to 'bring football home' since the male team won the World Cup back in 1966, fifty-six years before.

Obviously, winning the Euros was a mad achievement – a big and unforgettable dream come true. But achievements come in all shapes and sizes. They're not just about winning trophies or medals, they can be small and meaningful too. Like when you beat your personal best in a sporting challenge or master a new skill or speak up about something that has been playing on your mind. These triumphs are medal-worthy too.

When I scored my first hat-trick for England's Lionesses during a World Cup qualifier against Latvia, I was able to keep the match ball and got it signed by everyone – a souvenir for life and a great record of my achievement. I keep it in my bedroom as a reminder. I think it's important to celebrate every single win, no matter how big or small.

You could do the same and keep a record of your own achievements. Why not create an achievement jar? Or a box of brilliance? Whatever you want to call it! It can be a way to collect the things you're proud of, whether they're giant trophies and certificates or pieces of art you've created. Or if your achievement is something that doesn't come with an item, write it down on a piece of paper and add it to a jar.

We should all be recording our achievements and remembering what we've done well. I hope doing this will help you stop self-doubt creeping in and allow you to focus on building your self-belief instead.

NIKITA

'There's something special coming,' whispered Phil Neville. It was early May, two months before his chosen squad would head across the English Channel to play football against the best teams on the planet in the 2019 World Cup in France. I looked at Phil, puzzled; I didn't understand what he was talking about.

The league had finished and some of the girls were doing extra training at Manchester City training ground to sharpen our skills. Suddenly, everyone started looking at their phones. The England squad was being announced by a bunch of different celebrities!

'Ha! DJ Monki just announced my place,' laughed Keira Walsh.

Before long, Prince William had announced that Steph Houghton would be on the plane to France. So would Fran Kirby, according to Ellie Goulding. And then it was my turn.

'Nikita Parris will wear the number 7 shirt,' announced David Beckham.

◢ DAVID BECKHAM! ◤

'Wow! Just . . . wow!' I said, over and over. I couldn't stop smiling. David Beckham, football icon and inspiration, who wore the number 7 shirt for England himself, just announced my place in the squad with that very same number. David watched our World Cup games with his daughter and later he told me that because of the number 7 on my shirt, I had become her favourite player. I felt so proud of myself for inspiring the next generation of young female football fans.

BELIEVE IN POSSIBILITY

When I was a little girl, I used to say to my mum, 'I'm going to play football for a living.' But she was worried that there would be no pathway for me to get there. At the time, there was no women's team like the men's team. But I knew that one day there would be.

The USA had a strong women's league and I'd seen my idols Kelly Smith and Karen Carney move to the States for their football careers. So when I was thirteen, I told my mum if I couldn't make it in England, I'd move to the States like them. I loved football so much, and all I wanted to do was play and progress. So if that was the only way I could do it, I would. If you're trying to get somewhere to achieve your dreams and the path is blocked, you might need to come back down the way you came and find an alternative route.

'THERE IS ALWAYS A PATH TOWARDS YOUR DREAMS — YOU JUST HAVE TO BELIEVE IN WHAT IS POSSIBLE.'

When I was eight years old, something happened that went on to completely shape my belief in what is possible. My mum brought home a film called *Bend It Like Beckham*. The main character was an eighteen-year-old football-mad British Indian Sikh living in London with her family. She was called Jesminder, Jess for short. In the film, she's invited by another girl, Jules, to join the local women's football team and she loves it! The problem is, her family want her to do more traditionally 'female' things, and they tell her she needs to quit football. (I won't ruin the ending for you in case you want to watch it!)

This film had a huge impact on me. It was the first time I'd seen other girls like me playing football. I watched it over and over again. In fact, I watched it so much that I wore the video out and eventually broke it! But it didn't matter – I'd already seen what was possible for myself.

I've now learned how important it is to believe in what's possible and to believe in your own potential to get there (we'll be coming back to this idea again in chapter seven). This belief in knowing you CAN do something is especially helpful when you're told that you CAN'T or that you SHOULDN'T or when things don't go your way.

Take life as a professional football player. You don't

always make the squad and, even when you do, you aren't always in the starting eleven. But it's still important to accept that even though things won't always go the way you hope they will, you still have the **potential** and the **ability** to achieve your goals.

That, for me, is what self-belief is all about – knowing that YOU CAN DO IT, even when you're not chosen or when things don't go to plan. So, whatever your goal is, just know that you can keep trying, and with determination and hard work it's POSSIBLE – that is what matters.

❝ YOU NEED TO BELIEVE IN WHAT'S POSSIBLE TO STAY MOTIVATED. ❞

For me, that belief in what's possible has taken me all the way. I went on to become the top goal scorer in the Women's Super League (WSL) between 2018 and 2020 and I'm proud to stay I'm still in the top-ten female goal scorers.

CONFIDENCE: REMINDING YOURSELF THAT YOU CAN

Playing at the sports court with my brothers and their male friends growing up took a lot of confidence. Some of them would try and make me believe that I wasn't any good, and the only reason I was allowed to play was that my brothers let me. But I knew that wasn't the case, so I would say: 'I've played plenty of games with my brothers in the garden. I've beat them, and now I'm ready to come and beat you!'

And I did. But I only had that confidence because I'd already proved I could play football with my brothers. I had proven that 'YES, I COULD' do this.

That inner confidence helped when I joined the Under-9s Kingsley United boys' team when I was seven years old. I'd already been playing football with the lads from the court since I was five. They were four or five years older than me and a lot bigger, but I was still winning games. Not all the games, but some. And my confidence grew each time I weaved the ball past the boys I was playing with.

That's how confidence works. It grows the more you do something.

CONFIDENCE OR COURAGE?

Sometimes you might decide against trying something even though you really want to, because you don't feel confident. But you should never let a lack of confidence hold you back.

Remember, confidence comes *after* you've done something, not before, so expecting to feel super confident *before* you try something can be a bit too much to ask of yourself. The more you practise something, the better you become and the more confident you feel. And this can take time.

To try something new (and to try something again after you've made a mistake), what you actually need is **courage**. You need courage to take those first steps and give something a go. And you need courage to do something again if it didn't go well the first time.

With everything you've done in your life, there was once a time when you'd never done it before. There was a time when you had never stood on your own two feet and walked before, but then one day you took your first step, then another. You probably fell down (I think we all did!), but you got back up and tried again until, before long, you were walking from one side of the room to the other . . . and now look at you!

> CONFIDENCE COMES FROM KNOWING YOU CAN DO IT BECAUSE YOU HAVE THE PROOF, BECAUSE YOU'VE DONE IT BEFORE.

> COURAGE COMES FROM NOT KNOWING WHETHER YOU CAN DO SOMETHING WELL, BUT GIVING IT A GO ANYWAY.

So, how do you find courage?

COURAGE: NAVIGATING NERVOUSNESS AND DEALING WITH PRESSURE

Nobody feels brave or confident all the time. Even when you're a pretty confident person, scary situations or important events can still make you nervous.

For me, it's walking out on to the pitch for a World Cup game or the pressure of taking a penalty. For my first World Cup in France, England's first game was against Scotland, and I felt very nervous. I'd played big games before, but this was the biggest game I'd ever played. I needed courage and lots of it. So I made a plan.

The plan was to try and have a good first pass and keep to the basics for the first ten minutes (like dribbling the ball and staying in good passing range), to ease myself into the game.

Later in the game it became tighter and faster, and there was a point where I said to myself, 'Right, now it's time to start taking more risks, be more creative and get into the game.' So that's what I did. I started to take braver chances, and became more attacker-minded. And it worked out: everything went according to plan.

I even scored a penalty and won Player of the Match!

And it's the same with penalties. It's nail-biting enough when you're watching at home. Imagine what it feels like to step up to that spot and take a penalty – when all eyes are on you, when the hopes and dreams of all the supporters, sometimes the whole country, are relying on you. It won't surprise you to hear that this is a lot of pressure!

Whenever I step up to take a penalty, the pressure builds gradually as I'm carrying the ball, and when I'm putting it on the spot. But as soon as I decide which way I'm going, and remind myself that this is something I've practised many times before, that's when I become free.

The moment you start to have indecision, or doubt yourself – that's when you allow pressure to creep in. But deciding on a plan of action (in my case, which way I'm going and where I aim to put the ball) reduces that pressure and gives you courage.

For me, with penalties, I always take four steps back and one or two steps wide of the ball. That's just a process I go through that makes me more comfortable in my accuracy and gives me the courage I need.

Having a plan and a process and slowly easing into whatever you're doing are great ways to navigate your way through nerves and build your courage. And then, the more you do it, the more confidence you will gain.

THE THREE Ps: POSSIBILITIES, PLANS AND PREPARATION

Pressure (in penalty taking, in matches and in life) usually comes from other people's expectations – coaches, teachers, parents, fans, classmates – and from not wanting to let those people (or yourself) down. But this can mean you end up putting *too* much pressure on yourself. How much pressure you feel will depend on how much courage and confidence you have, and how much you allow all the outside noise to affect you.

For me, the best way to turn down the outside noise is by remembering the three Ps – possibilities, plans and preparation. So, here's a little reminder:

1. POSSIBILITIES: remember to believe in what's possible.

2. PLANS: have a process – plan beforehand the steps you can take to help you feel more comfortable and courageous in the moment.

3. PREPARATION: keep practising. This way, when you come to do the hard thing, you can give yourself a confidence boost, by reminding yourself that you've done this many times before, and it can be done.

NIKITA'S NIFTY NOTES ON PERFECTING THE THREE PS

Imagine you're in a situation where you need to focus on the three Ps. For example, let's say you need to present in front of your class and you're feeling nervous.

★ First of all, remember that you CAN do it. You have to believe in the possibilities. Other people in your class have done this before, and they were totally fine. There's no reason you can't do this too!

★ What's your plan of action? It might include reading through your presentation in your head, then reading it out loud on your own. Next you might read it to a trusted grown-up, and then, once you're feeling more confident, read it again.

★ Ask yourself, what will I do if I fall down or mess this up? Prepare for that too (see chapter eight). For example, plan what to do if you end up speaking too fast, or stumbling on your words. Your plan might be to take a deep breath and carry on.

★ PRACTISE, PRACTISE, PRACTISE.

By the time you deliver your presentation to your classmates, you'll have far more courage than if you hadn't prepared. And afterwards, your confidence will be sky-high because **YOU DID IT**!

Believing in yourself and knowing you've got the capability to do something comes from practising, training, failing, learning, improving and growing. So, keep going. Persist! As the saying goes:

"IF AT FIRST YOU DON'T SUCCEED, TRY, TRY AGAIN."

GEORGIA

It was a school day like any other, or so I thought. I was a bit late getting home that day, and as I walked into the living room, there he was – Nick Cushing, the manager of Manchester City Women's Football Club, sitting at the table, having a cup of tea with my mum, dad and brother.

He wanted to meet up to talk about my future.

Obviously, it was exciting to have a Women's Super League manager want to speak to me. But I didn't really think anything of it. At the time, I was playing for Blackburn Rovers and had just joined the senior squad. I'd scored a lot of goals in a short space of time and was loving it. But I certainly wasn't expecting Nick to be sitting in my living room any time soon!

We talked a bit about what my future could look like, and I remember asking him whether there might be an opportunity for me to train with the first team, or get exposed to them in some way?

Nick looked at me and a few seconds of silence followed. 'Why do you think I'm here, Georgia?' he said, smiling. 'I'm not signing you for the development team. I'm not signing you for the Academy. I'm here to sign you for the first team!'

Wait. *What?* I couldn't believe it. I was sixteen and still completing my GCSEs at the time. I could hardly contain my emotions. As soon as Nick left the house and got into his car, I ran up and down the stairs screaming!

It was all a bit of a whirlwind after that. I signed the contract to join Manchester City in July 2015, and a couple of days after finishing my last exam and leaving school, I moved out of my family home in Barrow-in-Furness and moved in with a host family who I didn't know, a hundred miles away in Manchester.

I'd been playing football for as long as I could remember. I started out in the garden with my three brothers. After this, I started to train with my brother's Under-7s team and played with Furness Rovers until I was twelve. Later, I persuaded my mum to take me to Blackburn Rovers,

a ninety-minute drive away, to trial for their girls' team.
And I continued playing for Blackburn right up until Nick
Cushing showed up in my living room and convinced me
to take on this brand-new challenge . . .

BOLD MOVES

Moving away from my family and home meant getting outside my comfort zone in a big way. But sometimes that is what you have to do to achieve your goals. I knew I needed to make this move because I loved football, and I had the opportunity to go to the best possible place to help build my career. And I soon found that getting outside my comfort zone did something else – it made my comfort zone wider. A little discomfort leads to a lot of growth, because you stretch yourself, and that's when you learn that you're capable of more than you thought you were. After this move, I felt more comfortable in new situations than I had done before, because my comfort zone had grown and so had I. And that gave me the confidence to keep stretching myself further.

I've since learned that psychologists call this attitude of embracing new challenges a 'challenge mindset'. It's all about knowing that the more challenges you take on, the more opportunities you have to prove to yourself that YES, YOU CAN do this! This builds your belief and confidence in your abilities, which makes it easier to take on new challenges in the future.

Change often feels uncomfortable because of the uncertainty that comes with it. Not knowing what's going to happen or how things are going to turn out can make change feel a bit scary. But change brings with it so many possibilities for growth and progress. And if you refuse to embrace change or try something new that makes you a little uncomfortable, you'll never know the heights you could reach.

Imagine your comfort zone is a bubble. Inside it is everything and everyone you know and love and are used to. What's in **your** comfort zone? Now, don't get me wrong. Having a comfort zone is so important. It contains all the things that already bring you joy. But if you stay inside your comfort zone forever, in a bubble surrounded by everything familiar to you, you won't try anything new, difficult or exciting. So yes, you'll stay comfortable, but you'll never know the person you could be if you stepped outside that bubble and tried something new.

When I moved so many miles away from home, there were obviously times when I just wanted a hug from my parents and to have my family around me, especially after a frustrating training session, after losing a game or if I was feeling ill. But if I hadn't taken that bold move, I wouldn't have had the opportunity to play for the Manchester City first team and then for England, a dream I'd had since I was a little girl.

A short while after sixteen-year-old me moved to Manchester, I met the rest of the team. There were players such as Steph Houghton and Jill Scott, who'd been my idols growing up, sitting next to me in the Manchester City dressing room. It was surreal.

I didn't know then that I'd make 186 appearances in all competitions and win seven trophies with Manchester City, nor that I'd stay for seven years and leave as the club's record women's goal scorer with sixty-seven goals.

STRETCHING OUTSIDE MY COMFORT ZONE PAID OFF.

FROM ONE BOLD MOVE TO ANOTHER . . .

Moving away from home that first time made it easier to make another bold move again later in my career – to play for Bayern Munich, in Germany.

Don't get me wrong, moving even further away from friends and family to Munich at the start of the 2022–2023 season was difficult. I didn't speak the language or know anyone in the country. But I'm thriving! I love my life in Munich and my football has improved too. Here I am living in a completely different city with people I've only known a short while, but they're a massive part of my life now. What felt uncomfortable at first is now very, very comfortable.

BY CONTINUING TO STEP OUTSIDE MY COMFORT ZONE, IT HAS STRETCHED WIDER AND WIDER, AND THIS HAS SHOWN ME THAT I CAN FACE NEW CHALLENGES WITH COURAGE AND CONFIDENCE.

GEORGIA'S GREAT GUIDE TO STRETCHING YOUR COMFORT ZONE

★ Think about a big dream of yours.

★ Is there a step on the pathway towards this dream that feels a little uncomfortable? It could be talking to people you don't know, or going on a trip that means you'll be away from home for a while, or simply doing something you've never done before.

★ Now picture that uncomfortable step as a slightly spiky rung on a ladder or a thin plank on a wobbly bridge. If you take it away, you can't climb the ladder or cross the bridge and you'll be stuck where you are – comfortable but not moving forward in the direction of your dreams.

★ Now imagine how good and brave and confident you'll feel after taking that difficult step and getting closer to your dream. See yourself climbing the ladder or reaching the other side of the bridge, having experienced the discomfort but getting where you wanted to go.

★ Use that visual image as a way to spur you on during times of discomfort, to remind you that it's worth it to achieve your goals and reach your dream destination.

Be courageous like a Lioness. Throw yourself into opportunities, even if they feel big and scary. Say yes to discomfort and uncertainty. Be open to feeling a bit weird. If I'd have said 'no' to moving to Manchester or Munich, I'd never have known how far I could go.

I CAN AND I WILL - WATCH ME!

Remember at the start of this chapter, when Tooney shared how the belief of her family and fans has bolstered her belief in herself? It's the same for all of us. Keets's family have travelled the country and abroad to support her, and my mum drove me on a three-hour round trip to Blackburn every week for four years so I could play football. She even put up with me firing footballs at her in the net every day during the summer holidays, because I needed to practise shooting and scoring. My mum absolutely hated it, but she knew improving my scoring skills would help give me the confidence I needed.

Just as having people who *do* believe in you can give your confidence a boost, so can having people who don't. I know this sounds odd – how can naysayers (people who say you can't do something) help you believe that you *can*?

Well, I knew I wanted to be a footballer from when I was a young child wearing a too-big hand-me-down kit. I was an outdoorsy, energetic child, and my love for the game was so strong. Everything I did was for football. Every time I went to a party, I took a football. Every time I left the house, I had a football in my hand. The car was full of footballs.

But it wasn't until midway through secondary school that I knew, if I put in the work, I could potentially make a career out of it. Back then, it was very difficult to become a full-time professional footballer as a woman. Female players weren't paid enough to earn a living, so they needed to work other jobs at the same time. I wasn't sure what to do – I thought, *Should I just focus on something else and let football be in the background?*

But the turning point for me came after I went to a careers fair at school. I was about fourteen and my back-up plan if I didn't become a footballer was to maybe join the army or the police. I was walking around the careers fair looking at leaflets when a lady came up to me and asked, 'So, tell me, what do you want to be when you're older?'

' I WANT TO BE A PROFESSIONAL FOOTBALLER. '

I replied immediately. She gave me a look of disbelief.

'Well,' she said, 'you're going to have to start playing for a team sometime soon then.' She didn't know that I was already playing for Blackburn Rovers, but I could see she doubted me – she clearly didn't think I could do it!

This made me think to myself, *OK, I'm gonna show you!*

It was at this point that I knew I wanted to prove to everyone that it's possible. I wanted to make the women's game as big as it could be, and do my community proud.

So, you see, when someone says you can't do something, that can spur you on and give you an extra dose of determination to prove them wrong: to prove what you can do and show them what's possible. To say, 'I can, and I will – watch me!'

CHAPTER THREE: SELF-CARE IS HEALTH CARE

GEORGIA

Caring for yourself is *so* important for both your physical health (the way your body feels) and your mental health (the way your mind feels). And self-care is more than just soaking in a nice hot bubble bath; it's all about tending to your own needs. It's about checking in with yourself and knowing when you need to take a step back, reflect on how you're feeling, and preserve your mental and physical energy. And yeah, sometimes it's easier to just focus on working super hard and trying to do ALL THE THINGS, ALL THE TIME.

BUT SELF-CARE DECISIONS ALLOW YOU TO PROTECT YOUR MENTAL AND PHYSICAL HEALTH, SO YOU CAN SHOW UP AS YOUR BEST SELF AS OFTEN AS POSSIBLE!

GROWING PAINS

I remember a time in my career when I was struggling to play my best football and was finding it hard to balance training full-time with my schoolwork. I was seventeen, and it was a year since I'd first joined Manchester City. I had just started to feel settled, but then puberty hit. We all go through this stage of growing up at different times. Unfortunately, for me, it all happened in my first year as a professional footballer – just when I was trying to find my way and balance everything on my own for the first time, having just moved away from home.

I was at that stage of growing up where my body was changing, growing and filling out, and my mood was swinging all over the place due to the hormones racing around (more on those later). I was lacking motivation and energy, and obviously not playing my best football! This meant I wasn't always included in the squad, so I was getting less game time, which reduced my fitness level, which impacted my performance, which affected my mood, my motivation, and my attitude even more. I was questioning why I was there, asking myself what was going wrong.

One day, after I'd been at the club for a year, the manager called me into a meeting. Although he could see I was a big talent with a big future ahead of me, he'd noticed I wasn't playing my best football and told me there and then that something needed to change.

Sometimes football clubs give their players the option to go out on loan to another team (so another club borrows you for a while), and he told me, 'You've got until Friday to decide whether you want to go out on loan or not.'

That was a big wake-up call. Ten minutes after leaving his office, I phoned my agent. 'I'm not going,' I declared. 'I'm going to fix this.' And in that moment, I flicked my determination switch back on.

❛ I KNEW I NEEDED TO KNUCKLE DOWN AND SWITCH ON, SO THAT'S WHAT I DID. ❜

I thought carefully about how I could care for my mind and body, to boost my energy and get myself feeling happier and performing better. I started to eat healthier, drink more water, go to bed earlier and exercise more. I learned what gave me energy and what drained it.

Soon I noticed that my energy levels began to rise. This gave me the motivation I needed to balance my school-work and my training more effectively. My head felt clearer, and within a couple of months, I'd got everything back under control.

This was such an important lesson for me.

IF YOU WANT TO KEEP BEING YOUR BEST SELF, YOU NEED TO TAKE CARE OF YOURSELF. OTHERWISE YOU WON'T HAVE THE ENERGY TO FIND THE MOTIVATION YOU NEED TO KEEP GOING!

VERY SUPERSTITIOUS . . .

Have you heard how some football players have superstitions about what they like to do before a match for good luck? For example, David Beckham always made sure his fridge was tidy before a match, Ronaldo felt luckiest placing his right foot on to the pitch first, Leah Williamson always has a bath on game day and Alessia Russo always puts on her right sock, boot and shin pad before her left!

My superstition was to eat baked beans! That super-stition has changed now (because I can't get that brand of beans in Germany where I now play!). But it used to be that before a game, I would always eat beans on toast as my go-to energy boost and good-luck charm combined. It's just a simple routine that helped me feel good.

But that isn't my only method of self-care! I always try to control my energy levels with how much I train and sleep, and my water and food intake, which are like fuel.

TAKING CARE OF YOUR BODY IS ONE OF THE KEY STEPS TOWARDS TAKING CARE OF YOUR MIND.

You might be thinking, *But these are all things that impact your physical health! What about your mental health?!* Well, your physical and mental health are actually far more connected than you might realize.

YOUR HORMONE TEAM

Hormones are chemical messengers in the body. It's through these hormones that our body and brain constantly communicate.

When we go through puberty, our brains release a special hormone, which kick-starts the changes our bodies go through. This then causes the release of more puberty hormones. For boys, this process triggers the production of a hormone called testosterone, and for girls it's a hormone called oestrogen. All these changes inside our bodies not only affect how we look physically, but also how we feel.

But it's not just puberty hormones that affect how we feel – we have lots of other hormones that impact our mood, no matter what age we are. This is why it's useful to get to know and understand how our hormones work, what triggers them and what we can do to release more of the hormones that make us feel good.

Let's imagine our hormones as team members in a six-a-side football team.

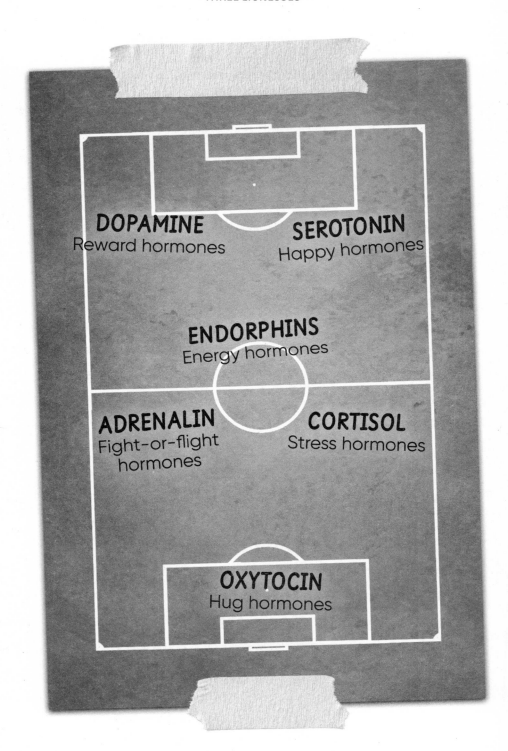

Serotonin, dopamine, oxytocin and endorphins are nicknamed 'feel-good hormones' because they can impact our mood positively. So it makes sense to focus on them – or get the ball to these happy hormones.

Other hormones, such as adrenalin and cortisol, are 'stress hormones', which come in to play when we face stressful situations. They trigger responses that prepare you to tackle an emergency and defend yourself.

Each 'player' has a job to do, and, when they work together as a team, the game goes well. But if any of them get carried away and take over, hogging the ball without passing to their teammates, those players take control of the game, and the lack of balance can make everything go awry.

For example, adrenalin triggers the 'fight-or-flight' response. This is the body's natural reaction to real or imagined threats of danger, where our breathing and heart rate quickens and our blood pumps faster so we can respond quickly to the danger. Fight-or-flight is a built-in survival instinct which kept our ancestors alive by putting them into a state of hyper-awareness so they could either fight or run away from the danger. This is why a small amount of adrenalin can increase your concentration, alertness and performance during an emergency, but too much adrenalin can trigger anxiety and restlessness.

Cortisol usually balances our body's health and our appetite in a positive way. But when the stress response is activated, cortisol spikes to put the body on high alert, which shifts focus away from those tasks and towards tackling the stressful situation. For short periods, this is good because it drives the body into motion and helps us focus on the problem at hand. But if cortisol hogs the ball and stays on high alert for too long, those higher levels can make us feel tired and lose focus, which can impact our body's health.

So it's helpful to be aware of which hormone is hogging the ball, so you can win it back, gain more balanced possession and keep the game running smoothly. In a way, we have to be like the referee. If we notice ourselves feeling stressed or anxious, we need to blow the whistle, pause and figure out what to do next to create a more balanced game.

Let's look at each of these 'players' in a bit more detail, so we can understand their role, and what we can do to get them back into the game when they're on the bench (or give them a red card when they need to be sent off!).

DOPAMINE

POSITION: ATTACK

PURPOSE: Reward and motivation

DOPAMINE COMES OFF THE BENCH WHEN: you experience something pleasurable, like smelling a chocolate cake baking. Or accomplish something, such as scoring a goal for your team or completing a level on a computer game. It's released as a reward to motivate you to repeat whatever gave you that feeling.

This is useful when it pushes you to go after your goals, but it can also make you want to play level after level of a computer game or keep eating more and more slices of cake, which you need to watch out for!

If dopamine stays on the bench and doesn't get any game time, your mood can be negatively affected, making you feel down and demotivated. So, balance is important.

SEROTONIN

POSITION: STRIKER

PURPOSE: Mood-booster

SEROTONIN COMES OFF THE BENCH WHEN: you are exposed to sunlight or soil from the ground outside, or when you exercise.

When serotonin is benched, your mood goes down. But when serotonin gets game time, it can reduce both sadness and feelings of worry, and boost your mood in a positive way.

ENDORPHINS

POSITION: MIDFIELD

PURPOSE: The body's natural pain-reliever

ENDORPHINS COME OFF THE BENCH WHEN: you laugh, exercise, eat a delicious meal or fall in love!

Endorphins are the body's natural painkillers, and they also create a sense of general wellbeing.

OXYTOCIN

POSITION: DEFENCE

PURPOSE: To help us bond with each other; also known as the 'hug hormone'

OXYTOCIN COMES OFF THE BENCH WHEN: we hug or touch people we trust, listen to music or do some exercise. Oxytocin is also a good stress-reliever.

HOW TO GET THE HAPPY HORMONES OFF THE BENCH

★ Foods such as bananas, avocados, pumpkin seeds, sesame seeds, chicken, milk, cheese and yoghurt are good for releasing dopamine. (I wouldn't suggest eating them all at the same time, though, unless you like the idea of a mushy, seedy, cheesy banana and chicken platter?)

★ Watch the sunset, gaze up at a tall tree or watch a football game where one of the world's best players wows you – anything that makes you experience awe.

★ Write in a gratitude journal (like Tooney mentioned in chapter one).

★ Meditate. This involves sitting still, closing your eyes and focusing your attention on your breath. Each time your attention moves away from your breath and turns to a worry or other thought, bring your attention back to your breath over and over again. If you find this too hard, try listening to a guided meditation on an app (you could ask your parents to download one on their phone if you don't have one yet). Focusing your attention on your breath or the words you hear in a guided meditation can release dopamine, trigger endorphins, calm the mind and ease pain.

★ Get outdoors into the sunlight. During wintertime, or when there's less sunlight, our serotonin levels drop. But there are special lights you can buy that mimic sunlight, which you can use during the winter months.

★ Go for a walk with someone, ideally near woodlands or trees. Trees produce woody oils called phytoncides. Breathing them in sends a signal to your brain to switch from a stress response to a calm response, and swaps the cortisol and adrenalin production for serotonin and oxytocin – hello, happy hormones!

★ Get your hands dirty and plant something. The bacteria found in soil activates serotonin production.

★ Exercise causes your body to release serotonin. So playing football or any sport really can make you happier – especially if it's an outdoor sport, as then you're experiencing the benefits of nature and sunshine too!

★ Any kind of exercise will do, whether it's dancing, cycling or fast-walking, but one study found that high-intensity martial arts training can trigger a leap in oxytocin in particular. So get those karate kicks ready!

★ Playing musical instruments such as the drums or singing has been shown to release endorphins and increase how tolerant we are to pain.

★ Having a good laugh can release a rush of endorphins, as well as increasing our levels of serotonin and dopamine! So, laughter really is the best medicine. It's the same with smiling – even if you fake-smile, your brain can respond by releasing those happy hormones. Try it!

★ Don't hold back your tears if you need to cry. When we cry, both oxytocin and endorphins are released, which eases emotional and physical pain, and stress.

★ Singing in a group can release oxytocin and help you experience a sense of bonding. You could join a choir, a band or even just sit around singing your favourite

songs with a group of friends! The Lionesses love a good singalong on the coach to and from games. Especially Tooney! And it's no wonder us Lionesses were buzzing when we were singing 'Sweet Caroline' in the sunshine of summer 2022! (It may also have had something to do with winning the European Championship . . . !)

★ Give someone a hug (whether that's a human or a pet!). This releases oxytocin and gives you a warm fuzzy feeling, which has been shown to lower stress and anxiety.

ADRENALIN

POSITION: DEFENCE

PURPOSE: To provide energy and focus so you can react quickly in emergency situations

ADRENALIN COMES OFF THE BENCH WHEN: we feel under threat, or when something makes us feel scared, stressed, nervous or excited.

Adrenalin triggers the fight-or-flight response, which increases our heart rate and blood sugar levels and oxygen supply to the brain. This allows us to react quickly in response to danger. It comes in useful when we are facing a real danger or, for example, when we are playing football and need to react quickly to defend a goal or stop a pass. But adrenalin can also heighten levels of anxiety, so we need to balance it out.

PLAYER PROFILE

CORTISOL

POSITION: DEFENCE

PURPOSE: To regulate the body's stress response, and other important processes in the body

CORTISOL COMES OFF THE BENCH WHEN: we experience stress or anxiety.

Cortisol spikes during stressful moments and lowers when we're relaxed. When the fight-or-flight response is engaged, cortisol pushes the body's energy towards dealing with that situation, rather than doing its normal job. We don't want to keep cortisol away from doing its main job for too long, otherwise things like our appetites and our physical health would suffer. That's why it's good to find ways to reduce stress.

HOW TO GIVE CORTISOL AND ADRENALIN A RED CARD:

★ Go for a walk outdoors. Studies show that our cortisol and adrenalin levels reduce when we spend time around trees and nature.

★ Exercise. Research shows that physically active people tend to have a lower cortisol stress response than people who don't exercise.

★ Stay hydrated. Drink water as this will help you maintain healthy cortisol levels.

★ Eat more fruits and vegetables, especially leafy greens.

★ Practise deep breathing or meditation.

KEEPY-UPPYS

One of the best ways to learn ball control is by practising 'keepy-uppys'. You could call the activities that release feel-good hormones keepy-uppys too – they keep your mood up!

For example, Keets and Tooney are brilliant at making me laugh. Hanging out with them is a 'keepy-uppy' for me! I also like having a good tidy-up. It just makes me feel good, I'm not really sure why!

What are your keepy-uppys? What do you already do that makes you feel good? And what activities from the lists above could you do more of, now you know how great they can make you feel?

> **' TO BALANCE OUR HORMONES AND OUR FEELINGS, WE NEED TO FIND WAYS TO LIFT OURSELVES UP AND CALM OURSELVES DOWN. '**

HOW TO MAKE A 'CALM ME DOWN AND LIFT ME UP' BOX

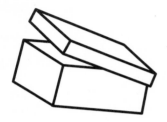

For times when it's not possible to get out in nature or play an instrument or do something else from the lists above, there are other things you can do to lift your mood.

You could make a 'feel-good' box that you store under your bed and get out whenever you need cheering up.

1. Get a shoe box and decorate it (that's a calming activity in itself!).

2. Place a selection of items inside, for example:

   ★ Bubble wrap to pop and tissue paper to crinkle. Both have a calming effect, because they distract the brain from stress.

   ★ A squishy toy, stress ball or some putty.

   ★ A colouring book and some pens.

★ A glitter jar, which you can make by adding glitter glue and food colouring to warm water and sealing. Shaking the jar and watching the glitter fall is distracting and calming.

★ A notebook to write thoughts in.

3. Write down effective calm-down/cheer-up activities on bits of paper and fold them up. You can then pick one, unfold it and do the activity. Options could include:

★ Take three deep breaths, slowly.

★ Make a bead bracelet using beads and elastic string.

★ Paint or draw.

★ Blow bubbles and then pop them!

★ Build a den with pillows, duvets and cushions.

★ Customize a water bottle then fill it up and drink from it.

★ Dance like nobody's watching.

★ Get and give three hugs (remember to ask a person if it's OK for you to hug them before you do it).

I'm going to hand over to Nikita here, because she has some excellent ideas about how to find calm, soothe worries and relax. (Keets and I are actually known as the Lionesses who can sleep anywhere, but we'll get on to sleep later!)

NIKITA

FROM WORRIER TO WARRIOR

When you're transferred to join a new football team, there are so many unknowns, and it's easy to create scenarios in your head of what might happen. And, because of that negativity bias that Tooney talked about in chapter one, those imagined scenarios always seem to be the worst possible ones.

That's how I felt when I joined French club Olympique Lyonnais on a three-year contract. I remember thinking, 'I'm just not sure if I can do this. I can't even speak French!' All I seemed to be able to do was imagine the worst.

Have you ever experienced that? Like when you're about to do something you've never done before, or are going to an event where you won't know anyone? The uncertainty about how it will go can make you feel nervous and anxious . . . can't it?

Whenever we're thinking about what *might* happen, we tend to overestimate what might go wrong and underestimate how well we'd cope even if it did. But I've found that when I actually go into the situation I've been worrying about, I'm often surprised because it never turns out to be like I expected. For me, it's always much better, easier and less scary than I thought it would be. All those worrying ideas about what I think could happen never actually come true!

Things are rarely as bad as you think they will be.

In Lyon, all the worst-case scenarios in my head disappeared very quickly. It turned out to be one of the best times of my career so far.

I think we often forget that with uncertainty comes POSSIBILITY. You never actually know what's going to happen because you can't predict the future, so instead of imagining what might go wrong, what if you try to imagine what might go *right*? Or even just remind yourself that it most likely won't be as bad as you imagine, and will possibly (probably!) be really GOOD!

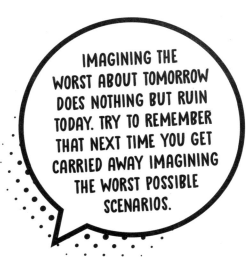

IMAGINING THE WORST ABOUT TOMORROW DOES NOTHING BUT RUIN TODAY. TRY TO REMEMBER THAT NEXT TIME YOU GET CARRIED AWAY IMAGINING THE WORST POSSIBLE SCENARIOS.

THE WORST, BEST AND MOST-LIKELY GAME

One way to stop ourselves imagining the worst is to play the 'worst, best, most-likely' game:

★ Think about whatever you're worrying about and imagine the worst-case scenario.

★ Now give that scenario a number out of ten for how likely you really think it is to happen.

★ Now repeat the process with the best-case scenario.

★ Now repeat it again with the most-likely-case scenario.

★ So, let's say you're worried about not being selected to join a new team at a football trial:

☆ The worst-case scenario is that not only do you not make the team, you play so badly that the coach makes a note on their pad that you'll never play for any team ever again for the rest of time. Let's give the likelihood of this situation a 1/10.

☆ The best-case scenario is that not only do you make the team, but you are SO INCREDIBLE that you're immediately fast-tracked to become a Lioness and guaranteed to play for England in every squad from now until you retire. Let's also give this a 1/10.

★ The most-likely-case scenario is that you will either play well and are selected to join the team, or that you might not be selected to join this time but you go away to practise, train and try again next year, and hopefully get selected then. I'd give that a solid 8/10!

It can be fun to find the least and most likely scenarios, and this helps you get perspective about what's most likely to happen (which is never as bad as you first imagine).

Of course, keeping an open mind can be tough when we're in worry mode, because our emotional brains often close our mind to solutions. We get all caught up in these worry spirals of 'what if I fail and never improve?' or 'what if nobody likes me?' or 'what if I hate it here?' or 'what if I've made a mistake and it's too late to change my mind?'.

When one worry leads to another, starting with a small 'what if . . .?' and growing into a big anxious feeling, it's like rolling a football around a snowy pitch – it picks up more and more snow, getting bigger and bigger until it's a huge snowball! That's why this kind of catastrophic thought process is sometimes called 'snowball thinking'.

STUCK IN EMOTIONAL MUD

When you are snowball thinking, it's hard to focus on anything else – especially not how to solve the problem you're worrying about!

You can imagine this as though you're stuck on the wrong side of the pitch. Think of your brain as a football pitch that is split in two. On one side is the lush green rational side and on the other is the muddy emotional side. Imagine the ball is on the emotional side at the moment, and the aim of the game is to get the ball over to the logical side of the pitch where the 'thinking' brain is.

THE LOGICAL PART OF THE BRAIN IS THE 'PRE-FRONTAL CORTEX', WHICH ALLOWS YOU TO THINK CLEARLY, BE RATIONAL AND PROBLEM-SOLVE.

THE EMOTIONAL PART OF THE BRAIN IS CALLED THE AMYGDALA, AND WHEN THAT'S ENGAGED IT CAN BE DIFFICULT TO ACCESS THE LOGICAL PART OF THE BRAIN.

The problem is, when we are worried or scared, it triggers our stress response, so guess who comes along? The adrenalin and cortisol players! They are controlling the game and working hard to keep the ball over on the muddier emotional side of the pitch.

Ultimately, there's only one way to win the ball back from the cortisol and adrenalin players – and that is to calm down. Once calm, we can think clearly and pass the ball over to the rational side of our brains where our minds are more open to possibilities and solutions.

BUT HOW CAN **I CALM DOWN?!**

KEEP CALM AND CARRY ON!

I know when someone tells you to calm down it can make you feel even more riled up. But knowing how to calm yourself down is a really useful strategy, whether you're worried about sitting an exam, speaking in public, going somewhere new or even stepping up to the penalty spot!

So how can you stay calm in the face of fear or anxiety? How can you manage your thoughts rather than let them manage you? Well, here's a few ideas:

★ USE YOUR HEAD

Try distracting your brain from dwelling on the worries and negative thoughts too much. You need to focus your mind on a task that uses your logical 'thinking' side of the brain rather than the 'emotional' side. Counting is a good strategy for this. You could count backwards from 100 in sevens (sounds impossible, I know!). Or try naming every schoolteacher you've ever had, then spell their names out. Do it backwards if it's too easy. If you're out and about, count the number of blue cars in the street or clouds in the sky and if you're indoors, try counting all the metal or wooden or red items you can see. Or watch a football match and add together the players' numbers on their shirts!

★ USE YOUR BREATH

Before the World Cup in 2019, we talked as a team about high-pressure situations and how we could find brief moments ahead of stressful events to find calm – anything from thirty seconds to two minutes. One thing we all found helpful was to close our eyes and take deep breaths. Before stepping up to take a penalty, or a throw-in, or a corner, or anything where all eyes are on you, something really useful to do is to take five seconds to inhale, and five seconds to exhale.

Try it now for a few breaths and see if you notice anything – have your shoulders relaxed? Does your mind feel calm and clearer?

HOW TO USE BREATHING TO GET CALM

For me, I find it useful at half-time to take a minute to breathe slowly before responding to whatever's happened in the first half. It means I give a more open and honest assessment rather than an emotional reaction. There are loads of ways to use your breath to calm down. Turn the page for some methods you could try.

Count as you breathe and make the out breath longer

Breathe in through your nose to the count of four. Hold for a count of four, then breathe out through your mouth for a count of six. Counting as you breathe in and out makes it easier to focus your mind on your breath, and slowing your breathing and taking a longer out breath helps you relax.

Stop. Look Up. Breathe (SLUB)

If you're rushing from one activity to the next, stop what you're doing for sixty seconds, look up and breathe deeply in and out. This opens your chest and triggers your relaxation response. A friend of a friend calls this quick calming strategy SLUBbing.

Alternate nostril breathing

Hold one nostril down and breathe in. Release that nostril, hold the other one, and then breathe out. Then swap over. Did you know we breathe more heavily from one nostril than the other? I didn't either, but it turns out that this ancient method strengthens the connection between the right and left side of the body and the brain, balancing out our breathing and calming us down.

Diaphragmatic breathing

Place your hand on your stomach and picture a balloon inside. Imagine it expanding every time you breathe in and deflating when you breathe out. This helps you use your diaphragm (the major breathing muscle below the lungs) when you breathe and take fuller, calming breaths.

Say affirmations as you breathe

After you inhale, say 'I am calm'. After you exhale, say 'All is well'. This can help focus your mind as you relax.

★ USE MINDFULNESS MEDITATION

We often spend so much time worrying about what might happen in the future or what has happened in the past that it gets in the way of enjoying what's happening now. Mindfulness is all about shifting your focus away from the past or future, and into the present.

Lots of people think mindfulness meditation is about switching off and emptying your mind. It isn't though, really – it's more about switching on to what you are experiencing in the moment. It's a useful tool to have in your kitbag because it helps you get calm, slow down and make good decisions.

HOW TO PRACTISE MINDFULNESS

Focus your attention

Pay attention to your breath or your senses, or whatever you're doing in that moment. Actively think to yourself 'I'm breathing in' as you inhale and 'I'm breathing out' as you exhale. Take in your surroundings. What can you see in this moment? What noises can you hear? Say in your head 'I can see . . .', 'I can hear . . .' and finish the sentences. Your senses connect you to the moment, so this is a good and easy way to become mindful of what's happening right now.

Notice your attention wandering and bring it back

If you find your mind drifting away from your breath or your senses and surroundings, actively bring your thoughts back to the present moment. At first you'll probably notice your brain jumping from one thought to the next. But by practising bringing your attention back, over and over again, you are meditating and being mindful. That's it, really.

All these different techniques are designed to help you feel calmer. Something might work well for one person, but not for you. And you might find practising mindfulness pretty easy, whereas someone else may struggle. There's no right or wrong. Just find whatever works for you and use it to help yourself feel happier and more relaxed!

UNPLUG: THE IMPORTANCE OF REST

'Nikita Parris sent home from England training camp over workload concerns' read the headline in the newspaper. It was November 2021, and we were due to play a World Cup qualifier against Latvia the next morning. I was a forward at Arsenal at the time, and the weekend after the Latvia game, we were going up against Chelsea in the FA Cup final. This was going to be followed by a Champions League group-stage match against Barcelona the following week. That's a lot of big matches in a row!

Football is an intense environment, and our manager Sarina gets it. She knows footballers need both physical and mental rest to keep up our energy, performance and wellbeing.

And it makes sense. If you overload a car and keep driving it at top speed and push it to its limit, you'll wear out the tyres and the engine. It will need refuelling (or recharging if it's an electric car). People need to take that time out to recharge and refuel too.

I'd had hardly *any* rest during this time. As a player, you often don't know when to stop, and many of us would probably just keep going and going if we didn't have a supportive team around us. We'd end up getting more and more tired and not performing well or improving as a result.

Often, when you're really busy, you think 'I don't have time to rest, I'm too busy to stop'. But in fact, that's when you need to rest and recharge the most!

For me, it was such a relief when Sarina gave me a physical and mental break. We talked with the medical staff, they listened, and together we decided that I should have four full days of rest. And wow, those four days off were just what I needed. I completely switched off from everything. I didn't watch any football. I didn't go on social media. I took myself away from London (which in my head was the 'football zone') and I went home to Liverpool to spend time with my family. This made me feel so free – like I could finally breathe. And do you know what? I didn't think about football once for the whole time!

Going forward, my decisions in football will always be based on balance. I now realize how important balance is in looking after yourself, giving you an energy boost, making you feel calmer and happier and ultimately helping you get better at what you do.

Can you think of a time when you've felt overloaded, or when you've had too much to do (homework, after-school clubs, school, music lessons, replying to messages, socializing)? It can feel overwhelming and exhausting, can't it? Choosing to rest in between all this activity can have a hugely positive impact! A well-rested brain is sharper because rest gives our brains the chance to process all the information we've taken in and everything we've been doing, and then concentrate on the next task. (That's why this state is called 'rest and digest' as opposed to 'fight or flight'.)

NIKITA'S NIFTY NOTES ON RELAXATION

Here are some things I find helpful when I'm looking to relax and recharge my batteries. I hope these might help you refuel too!

★ **Unplug, literally**

The average person looks at their phone up to 150 times per day, which means the brain is being constantly stimulated. By creating technology-free moments in your day (I mean no phone, no game console or computer screen, no TV – nothing), you can switch off and give your brain time to recover and recharge properly.

★ **Take tiny breaks from homework, revision or other work to boost concentration**

I like to nap every day if I can. But if I can't nap, I'll try to find little pockets of time for rest and relaxation. You can either SLUB (see page 138), or why not try the Pomodoro Technique? Developed by Francesco Cirillo in the late 1980s to avoid 'burnout' from overworking, the Pomodoro Technique suggests doing short bursts of focused work, broken up with five-minute breaks. So, you choose a project, set a timer for twenty-five minutes and focus fully on the task until the timer reminds you to take a five-minute break. Every four 'Pomodoros', you take a longer twenty- to thirty-minute break (ideally outside). As well as giving you time to relax, this tactic is also meant to improve your focus.

★ Listen to music

For me, listening to relaxing songs calms my brain, and listening to upbeat songs gears me up for big games. It's amazing the effect music can have on your mood and your energy – whether you need calming down or lifting up. And it helps me after games too! Playing football is intense, and you can feel high or low after, depending on the result. So after a match I'll take a moment to sit at my locker, listen to some music and reflect on what just happened.

★ Go for a walk outdoors

As Georgia said earlier in the chapter, walking outside in nature, especially if you are near trees, can calm you down as you breathe in the woody oils. Getting plenty of fresh air can help you sleep better too.

MY SLEEP ROUTINE

Talking of sleep, Tooney, G and I all need a minimum of eight hours' sleep per night, otherwise we're irritable and grumpy! Getting enough rest and a good night's sleep are both so important to give you the energy you need to feel your best, aim high and pursue your goals.

For me, sticking to a routine definitely makes sleep easier, and so does creating a calm environment. My wind-down routine starts an hour before I want to fall asleep. I'll start by listening to sounds of the ocean, rivers or rain via a meditation app or online video. That really helps me feel ready for bed. Although I listen on my phone, I try not to look at the screen. Instead, I shut my eyes, tuning in to those calming sounds of nature.

WHAT SOUNDS DO YOU FIND SOOTHING? COULD YOU FIND A WAY TO LISTEN TO THEM BEFORE YOU GO TO BED?

EMOTION IN MOTION

There's one more form of self-care that we want to talk to you about. And that's expressing your emotions. When you go through something difficult, you need to feel before you can heal. What I mean is that it's better to express your emotions and get them out, rather than keep them bottled up.

Imagine your emotions are emojis (little yellow icons showing different expressions) and each time you cry, the little crying emoji is released from your body. Or whenever you feel frustrated and do some exercise to calm down, the angry red-faced emoji is let out. Now, imagine if you never expressed your emotions – you kept your tears in and didn't express your frustration – the emojis would fill your body until one day you were fit to burst! Then they would all come flooding out in one big yellow mess. It wouldn't be pretty. It's so much better for you to express emotions when you feel them.

You can express your emotions in different ways. I find that kicking a ball is a good way to release anger or frustration in a healthy way. So does Tooney. She says she whacks the ball so hard it feels like she's whacking all the anger out of her.

Perhaps you're the same! Or maybe you'll feel better from confiding in friends and family about how you're feeling, or pouring it all out into a journal. Tooney does this too. She says that getting things off her chest and writing them down has really helped her, as she can just get everything out on paper and then forget about it.

Naming and labelling your emotions is another strategy that can take the sting out of them. Researchers found that saying 'I feel angry' or 'I feel sad' reduces the intensity of that emotion. However you choose to do it, it's always better out than in.

‟ WHAT ALL **THREE OF US** KNOW FOR SURE IS THAT IN ORDER TO GO AFTER **YOUR DREAMS**, YOU HAVE TO TAKE GOOD **CARE OF YOURSELF** FIRST! "

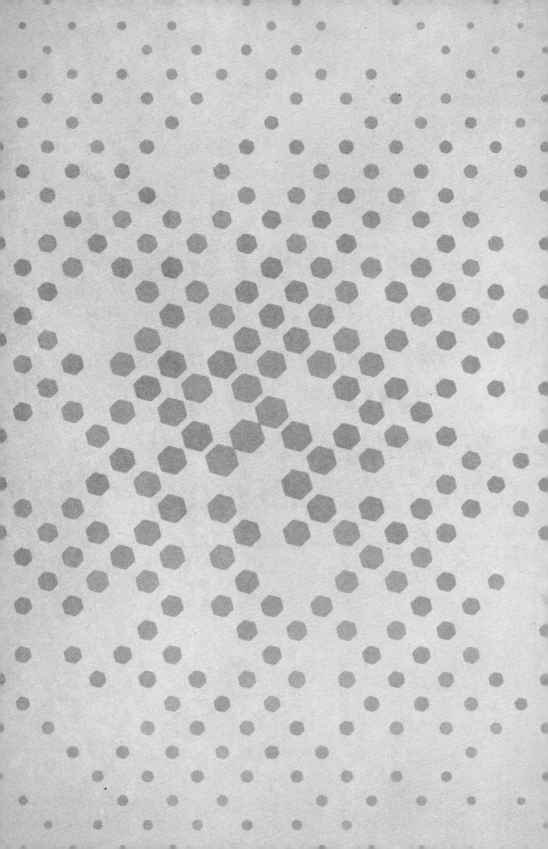

PART TWO
SHE SHOOTS

CHAPTER FOUR: SQUAD GOALS

ELLA, GEORGIA AND NIKITA

Did you know that in the wild, lions are the only cats who live in groups (or prides)? And that those prides are led and dominated by lionesses? (Ninety-nine per cent of the pride are actually related females. So, although we usually say 'a pride of lions', it would actually be more factually correct to say 'a pride of lionesses'!) Young male lions tend to come and go, leaving the pride at around two to three years old, while the female lionesses stick around and do most of the hunting for their cubs.

Lionesses stick together, and their pride is basically a sisterhood. They are fiercely supportive of each other, have each other's backs and hunt together to achieve the best results.

On the football pitch, as England's Lionesses, we're a supportive sisterhood too. We each have our own individual roles in the team, and we work together to get the result we all want – to win! As Lionesses, we take pride in our pride, so, in this chapter, we're going to explore finding your team and being a team player.

And it's all about quality, not quantity. So it doesn't matter whether your pride is a team of two or a much larger squad. It's how good these friendships and relationships are that will have the greatest impact on your mental health and wellbeing, and help you feel ready to go after your goals.

And unlike the other chapters in this book, where we've told you about our individual experiences, we decided to write this chapter together, as a team – because no Lioness is complete without her pride!

🪶 SO, ARE YOU READY FOR THE TEAM-TALK? LET'S HUDDLE. 🪶

WHY OTHER PEOPLE MATTER

As footballers, working as part of a team helps us to win games, trophies and championships, but it also makes us feel great, because good company is good for us.

In 1939, Harvard University began working on a study that is still going today. Researchers have found loads of evidence showing that supportive relationships reduce stress and are a massive source of satisfaction. Having a person or group of people to rely on and confide in relaxes us, keeps our brains healthier and gets us feeling happier. No wonder we love running around a football pitch with our teammates so much!

This is why 'social health' is such an important part of our overall mental health. According to psychologists, good social health is when you feel like you belong (to a family, to a team or to a community); when you have something in common with others; when you feel like you can add value to a group or to society in some way, and when you generally believe in the goodness of other people.

Also, having just one or two supportive relationships creates a kind of protective bubble around you when you experience something difficult. So, the more you can build and maintain your support squad, the better it is for your overall resilience (which we'll talk more about in chapter eight).

OUR FOUR FOUNDATIONS OF FRIENDSHIP

Whenever you build anything – a house, a support network, a relationship – you need firm foundations to build it on. Without this strong base, the house would just come tumbling down as soon as any bad weather hit!

Although there are all sorts of relationships that can help you feel good, happy and supported, we want to talk to you about the special relationship the three of us share – our friendship! We had a chat about what we see as the foundations of a good, strong, healthy friendship, and came up with this list:

1. Enjoyment

It's important to enjoy being in each other's company. This can mean lots of fun and laughter, or simply just quietly enjoying being together.

2. Trust

This is massive when it comes to building strong relationships, and it goes both ways. You need to be reliable, honest and loyal for people to confide in you, and you need to find people you can trust too.

3. Understanding

Everyone wants to feel seen, heard and understood. We want people to 'get' us, and other people need to feel like we understand them too. Understanding can be built by listening, by recognizing and accepting people's differences, and by empathizing, which means putting yourself in another person's position and understanding how they feel.

4. Support

We need people who lift us up when we're down and celebrate with us when things are going well. And we must give that same support back to others too.

We believe that with these foundations, no matter what challenges or stormy weather come our way, our friendship can withstand anything. Throughout this chapter, we'll be talking about how to build great friendships and relationships, and you'll see these themes of enjoyment, trust, understanding and support popping up a lot, so keep your eyes peeled!

THE GIFT OF A TEAM

We're all part of lots of different teams – we have a family team, a Lioness team, a team or community of football fans, and much more. Being part of a team is valuable. It brings:

★ shared moments, milestones and memories;

★ a sense of belonging and understanding;

★ someone* to confide in and trust;

★ someone to laugh and have fun with;

★ someone who brings out the best in us;

★ someone to help us get up if we fall down.

*This could be one person in the team, a few people or even the entire team.

Before we look at this in more detail, it's your turn! Think about the different teams you're a part of – perhaps you belong to a drama group, or a chess team, or a sports team – or maybe your family is your favourite team of all! What do you get from being a part of a team? Is there anything you'd add to the list above?

SHARING MEMORIES

Throughout the Euros in 2022, we had our Lioness pride around us everywhere we went. So every special moment, every difficult day, every funny memory and every challenge was shared with an amazing and supportive team.

And it wasn't just the other Lionesses we had around us. Our families and friends supported us everywhere we played. This meant they were there during the final match at Wembley to share a moment and milestone that none of us will ever forget. (Erm, did we mention that we won the European Championship?)

That win didn't just make our team of Lionesses proud; it made our inner circle of close friends and family burst with pride, and it made anyone who's ever known us (and even people we've never met) proud too. That shared moment of pride united us all and made a shared memory that will last in our hearts and heads forever.

'A HAPPY MEMORY FEELS EVEN MORE SPECIAL WHEN IT'S SHARED.'

Spending quality time with the people close to you is key to forming strong bonds and creating memories. We've all become pretty good at team building. We have group chats (the WhatsApp group for some of the girls who've risen up through the youth age groups is called 'Good Peeps'!), we go on dog walks, we go out for food and we enjoy lots of downtime together. Here are a few ideas for bonding activities to do with your own good peeps:

★ Get outdoors. Spend time together in nature or in a park.

★ Get active. Go walking, bike-riding, dancing or ice-skating together.

★ Ask a grown-up in your life to help you organize a trip together. You could visit the seaside, a zoo or a theme park.

★ Get crafty. Drawing, writing, knitting, building – these are all calming activities that can be even more fun when you do them with someone else.

When you get to play alongside your best friends, it means everything. For us, it's really special that we can go out on to the pitch and do what we love together. For Ella, sharing the pitch with Alessia Russo is such a mad experience because they've been friends since they were thirteen-year-olds, playing in the Under-15s. There's even a song about them!

❛ HERE WE GOOOOOO-OOO, TOONEY AND LESSI RUSSO! ❜

G and Tooney played at Blackburn together as fourteen-year-olds and hit it off right away. They soon found out that their parents went to school together! Later, when Georgia was in the transition between moving from her host family at Manchester City and finding somewhere else to live, she even lived with Ella for a bit, at the Toone family's home. One time, Ella's mum plaited Georgia's hair before a game and she went on to score a hat-trick. Ever since then, Tooney's mum says that the hat-trick was down to her plaiting!

These close relationships make the squad feel even more like a sisterhood. It's the same for Nikita, who loved playing for England alongside Fara Williams, Jill Scott, Demi Stokes and Toni Duggan because they'd grown up through the youth teams together, and Keets played alongside Lucy Bronze and Alex Greenwood at Lyon too. Having these shared experiences and these things in common has brought us all even closer!

GIVING OR RECEIVING AN 'ASSIST'

In football, when you pass to someone who then goes on to score, it's called an 'assist'. It was Nikita's assist that helped Georgia score a goal in her debut for the Lionesses' Senior Squad. It was October 2018, and we were playing Austria. Georgia was feeling nervous, and she wanted nothing more than to prove to herself and her teammates why she was there.

Luckily, she had a supportive team around her. About seventy minutes in, Nikita received the ball on the wing. She dribbled a bit, then cut the ball to the edge of the box, to where G was running. As G went to strike it, the ball came off her shin pad. Luckily, it went in the top right-hand corner of the net.

SHE SCORES!

Nikita's assist helped Georgia achieve her ambition of scoring on her debut. And Georgia's goal helped Nikita's stats too. It's special bonding moments like these that really bring us all closer together as teammates and as friends!

FINDING COMMON GROUND

Finding common ground with someone can be the foundation for a great friendship. It's like that for us in football. When you have someone who understands how it feels when things aren't going well and the joy when things *are*, it's great to have that person next to you on the journey. They just *get* it.

Think about the people close to you. Do you have things in common with them that have bonded you, or that make you feel more comfortable around them? Perhaps you're both new to a club or school. Or maybe you're both particularly tall or small (oddly, us three are exactly the same height – 5 foot 4 inches!). Or perhaps you have a mutual obsession with cats or football or a certain band. Perhaps you come from the same place? Or have been through a similar challenge as each other? Perhaps you're both good at football or maths or netball? Or you're both left-handed or left-footed?

Now, can you think of anyone you know who's not (yet) in your friendship group, pride or team (whatever you want to call it!), who you have something in common with? Perhaps you could try to get to know them better – what you have in common could be a good conversation starter. And you might find that a wonderful friendship starts to form!

SOMEONE TO CONFIDE IN

Nikita says that one of the best things that has happened to her in football is finding people she can confide in. It's important to have someone you can turn to.

According to research, having just one person you can confide in can be enough to keep loneliness at bay, because it means you feel seen, heard and understood – and that's something we all want really, isn't it?

When Ella was growing up, if she ever felt down or self-conscious, she would speak to people about it. She finds that getting things off her chest and letting it out always makes her feel better. She says, 'Once I get it out and I've said it, I don't dwell on it.' And that's the best thing about confiding in someone – you release your worries and frustrations, so they're not bottled up, festering.

Keets says when she was younger, she used to mask how she really felt rather than express her true feelings. Instead, she'd just smile and keep herself to herself. But ultimately, she'd end up feeling worse. She soon realized that in these moments, when you're feeling down or angry, having someone to lean on and to talk things through with can lift you out of your mood.

❝ SHARING IS CARING FOR YOURSELF. ❞

When you're going through hard times, it's important to find people with more experience or who understand what you're going through who can help you. It's much more difficult to navigate tough times when you try to shoulder them on your own.

But remember that people aren't mind-readers! You can't expect your friends or family to know what's going on inside your head unless you tell them. So when you feel ready, speak up and speak out because, ultimately, what others don't know, they can't see, and therefore can't help with. (We'll look more at *who* to talk to later.)

BE KIND AND SUPPORTIVE

Did you know that being kind has been proven to actually make YOU happier, and not just the person you're being kind to? Of course, being on the receiving end of a kind act makes you feel good. It's nice when people are nice to you. But researchers have also found that being kind sparks something called 'giver's glow' and releases those feel-good hormones. So cheering someone else up is a great way to cheer yourself up!

Kindness also encourages better teamwork because when someone's nice to you, it makes you more open to working with them as part of a team.

Here are some simple ideas for small acts of kindness that can make someone else's day – and hopefully yours too:

★ Remember when a friend has something important coming up (like a test or a competition) and wish them luck before it, or write them a card.

★ Write positive messages on pieces of paper, like 'you are amazing' and 'believe in yourself' and place them around your school or in library books. When people stumble across them, your kind words could cheer them up!

★ Compliment people. Perhaps they played well in a football match in the playground, or are wearing a nice outfit – no matter what it is, saying kind thoughts aloud is a great way to lift people's moods.

★ If you see someone on their own, go over and chat to them or invite them to hang out with you and your friends.

'IT'S NEVER A WASTE OF TIME TO BE KIND, NO MATTER HOW SEEMINGLY SMALL AN ACT OF KINDNESS IS.'

BE NICE TO NEWBIES

Before the Euros in 2022, G found out that she'd be joining Bayern Munich once the tournament was over. By the first day of the Euros, even though they were competing against each other in this tournament, lots of the Bayern Munich players had messaged G to say welcome to the club. These simple acts of kindness immediately helped G feel more comfortable and connected with these players who she would soon be joining.

Walking into a foreign changing room where you don't know anybody and where they're all speaking a different language to you is difficult. But when Georgia joined Bayern, she says it was like she knew everyone already, and the German players made her feel so welcome.

And Nikita felt exactly the same when she took that huge leap of faith by signing with Olympique Lyonnais. The team gave her such a warm welcome and went out of their way to make it as easy as possible for her to settle in. It was still hard, but their kind support really helped.

Wendie Renard, one of Nikita's new teammates, put her arm round her on one of her first days and reassured her by saying, 'It's OK, it takes time.' Even though she wasn't completely comfortable speaking English, Wendie still tried for Keets, and that meant a lot. The French girls would also translate what the coach said into English and then repeat it in French to help Nikita learn the language. Kind gestures like this not only helped Nikita understand more, but also helped her feel supported and gave her that all-important sense of belonging that drives us to connect with people.

> **HOW YOU MAKE OTHER PEOPLE FEEL IS AT THE HEART OF EVERY RELATIONSHIP. IT IS THE CORE OF ALL CONNECTIONS.**

Have you experienced what it's like to be a newbie? Maybe you joined a new school or club or team, or found yourself mixing with a new friendship group. Being new is difficult. Just like Wendie said, *it takes time!* And so when we're no longer newbies, and we see that someone else is in that position, it's our job to make them feel welcome. You can do this through your words and actions:

★ Don't just ignore new people because you don't know them – make them feel welcome with a smile or a fist-bump when they first arrive and invite them to join you and your friends. Be sure to say goodbye to them when they leave too.

★ Help them get to know others by explaining who else has recently joined. You could also introduce others with a description to help the new person get to know everyone. For example: 'This is Keets, she's the bubbly caring one', 'this is G, she's the joker of the group' and 'this is Tooney, she's fun and always up for a laugh'.

SUPPORTIVE SISTERHOOD

When you join a team as a younger player, there are often older team members who take you under their wing and look after you, like big sisters. Of course, just like real sisters, when you spend a lot of time together, you can sometimes wind each other up and annoy each other. Have you ever heard of 'sibling rivalry'? This is where you feel like you're in competition with your brother or sister, whether that's because you want to be better than them at certain things or even just to get more attention than them. This is quite natural, not only with siblings, but also with very close friends. However, it is always healthier, especially with friendships, to turn any rivalry and comparison into encouragement and inspiration.

> **A TRUE FRIEND WANTS ONLY GOOD THINGS FOR THEIR FRIENDS, AND WILL HELP TO BRING OUT THE BEST IN THEM, RATHER THAN TRY TO COMPETE.**

So if a friend runs faster than you, cheer them on! If they get a better mark than you on schoolwork, congratulate them. And if their jokes and stories are getting the biggest laughs, then laugh along too. If you support and encourage your friends when they do well, you'll hopefully find they do the same for you.

" LET'S BE SUPPORTIVE SISTERS RATHER THAN COMPETITORS. LET'S LIFT EACH OTHER UP RATHER THAN PUT EACH OTHER DOWN. "

UNITED

Female friendships can be a brilliant, beautiful thing. Women and girls are known to make strong, deep connections filled with open conversations, consistent care, empathy, encouragement and support. So although friendships can sometimes get complicated and stormy, navigating those storms is worth it because these special friendships are something to be treasured.

HAVING PLAYED FOR MULTIPLE TEAMS BETWEEN US THROUGHOUT OUR CAREERS, WE'VE NOTICED THAT THE BEST TEAMS HAVE A SPECIAL INGREDIENT THAT MAKES THEM STAND OUT—A SENSE OF UNITY, WHERE THE GIRLS GENUINELY WANT THE BEST FOR EACH OTHER.

When we all want to see each other do well, it makes such a difference. That feeling of pure pride you have for the person next to you outshines any feeling of competition. And ultimately that solid, supportive sisterhood makes our teams happier, stronger and perform better! That's squad goals!

There is one person who has always brought that sense of unity with her, and that's our former Lioness teammate Jill Scott. Jill has supported all three of us from day one, and she always gave us so much positivity and support. She did this by listening, encouraging, praising and lightening the mood. Jill is the best listener and is always someone you can talk to. But, more than that – you know she's got your best interests at heart. She doesn't see anybody as competition.

And that's important for a woman trying to succeed in football, as it has historically been seen as 'a man's world', where women were excluded. We need to help build each other up and remind each other that football is for *everyone*. To do this, we have to believe in ourselves *and* in each other.

'WHEN **IN DOUBT,** BE MORE **JILL!**'

STRENGTHENING YOUR FRIENDSHIPS

Let's be honest – friendships aren't always smooth sailing. There can be conflicts and disagreements, rivalry and other difficulties too. We've discovered that there are a few important things you can do to prevent arguments from happening and make sure that your friendships are strong, healthy and happy:

★ LOOK FOR THE COMPROMISE

Meeting in the middle is a good way to show your friend that you care about them. If you compromise on something this time, such as a snack to share or who does what in a presentation at school, someone else will compromise more next time. That's how good supportive relationships work – with give and take.

★ TAKE RESPONSIBILITY AND SAY SORRY

Apologizing when you've done something wrong is an important way to show the other person that you know and understand what you've done. When you apologize, you can start to move on from the situation.

★ LISTEN WELL

How do you listen well to others? First, focus on what they are saying, rather than thinking about what you want to say in reply. And make sure you wait for them to finish what they're saying rather than interrupting while they're talking. Then it might be that you can help them navigate their way through a challenge by sharing your own experience or suggesting someone they can talk to. Sometimes, though, it's more helpful to just stay quiet and listen. Being a shoulder to cry on is a good way to show support and give your friend a chance to say what's on their mind without interruption or judgement.

★ RESPOND WELL

How we respond to a friend's news is massive. A good friend is there to support you when you're struggling, but is also there to celebrate your successes! As we said above, if someone is sad, you can listen or offer words of comfort. Simply telling someone we hear them, we are there for them if they need us and that we wish they didn't have to go through this is sometimes all that's needed to show our support when they're low.

And how we respond to people when they share good news is just as important as our response to sad news. For example, when someone shares positive news about their life, some people might respond by either not showing much interest or turning the conversation back to themselves. So what *is* the best way to respond? The answer is something that psychologists call 'active constructive response'. You could say: 'Oh wow! That's exciting! How did you find out?' The aim is to get the good-news sharer to relive the experience and their excitement, so you can celebrate with them.

Just as offering comfort helps a sad friend feel less alone, offering enthusiasm helps a happy friend to enjoy their positive experience even more.

ACTIVE CONSTRUCTIVE RESPONSES

Imagine you've trained super hard and trialled for an exciting new team. Then you receive good news – you made it!

How do you think you'd feel if a friend responded with a disinterested 'cool' before going back to playing their game or scrolling through their phone? Or how would you feel if they said something negative like, 'Oh, but won't that be too hard for you? Won't you be too tired?' Or how about if they tried to compete with your achievement, and said something like, 'Oh, well, I've just signed to a new team too, but they're in the Extra-Major-Supersonic-League and they won last year and I . . .'

If anyone responds to your good news in this way, you'd probably feel the happiness and excitement draining out of you like a deflated football. So, to make sure you don't make anyone else feel that way, here are some examples of active constructive responses that you can say to share your friend's excitement with them:

★ Ask them how it felt. You could say, 'That's amazing! How did it feel when you heard the news?'

★ Ask them to tell you more about it. You could ask 'what happened next?'

★ Tell them how that makes you feel. For example, 'I'm so happy for you', or 'I'm so proud of you'.

TYPES OF SUPPORT: YOUR WORDS AND ACTIONS MATTER

The support you give to friends and loved ones can be physical or mental. An example of physical support is how Everton manager Mo Marley and her husband, Keith, used to go out of their way to drive Nikita to training and matches (which helped her become the player she is today). Mental support is more about the ways you care for your friends' mental wellbeing.

We think that these are three of the most important ways to support your friends mentally:

1. comfort and reassurance

2. encouragement and praise

3. empathy and understanding.

★ OFFER REASSURANCE

When it comes to reassuring someone, just a few little words can be massive for making their day feel brighter. As a footballer, playing in front of thousands of fans, with millions watching on TV at home and across the world, if you make a mistake, it can rattle you. When that happens, the encouraging words from the girls around you (the 'well done for trying', the 'don't worry, just keep going') has the power to settle your nerves and get you back on track.

Georgia remembers how she lost the ball in a game against the USA, and that resulted in the American team scoring a goal. She could have let that get to her, but our epic midfielder, Keira Walsh, went straight up to her and said, 'It doesn't matter. You're having an unbelievable game. Keep doing what you're doing. Keep getting on the ball.'

Then, as soon as we'd kicked off again, Keira gave the ball back to Georgia straight away. She wanted G to forget about what had just happened and to focus on the next thing. Five minutes later, Georgia took a penalty and scored!

★ OFFER ENCOURAGEMENT AND PRAISE

We all need positive encouragement from time to time when things aren't going our way. But equally, when somebody's doing something well, tell them! Thanks to that negativity bias (see chapter one), we may be more inclined to judge and criticize rather than compliment and praise. But if someone genuinely impresses you, why not let them know? This can help your friends feel more confident and will hopefully bring out the best in them.

★ EMPATHIZE

There's no 'I' in the word TEAM. There are so many different people in a team, and everybody has their own opinions and values and emotions. You soon learn it's not all about you, it's about what's best for the team. In football, you have to think: 'How can I make things better for everyone rather than just for me?'

When Keets moved from Everton to Manchester City, she learned to play football in a different way. At City, as well as knowing your own position, you needed to know your teammates' positions. This took her from thinking about the game from an individual perspective to thinking about how to get the best out of the players around her too.

That's also a useful strategy in life! When you can understand how other people see things (from a perspective that is probably different to your own) and consider their position, you can put yourself in their football boots and have more empathy for them. You can understand them better.

Say you want to go to the seaside with a group of friends, but one friend can't swim. The rest of you have your hearts set on going to the beach, so you could think about what's important to the non-swimmer. Maybe she really likes walking, so you could agree to all go on a long walk together before the rest of you have a dip in the sea. This way she gets to do something she'd enjoy first. You could also be conscious of the fact that she'll be sitting alone while you are in the sea, so you can all promise to take it in turns to sit with her. Or maybe she could be in charge of kicking a ball from the beach into the sea for you all to catch and throw back to her, so she's still involved?

BEING OPEN-MINDED TO OTHERS' EXPERIENCES AND FEELINGS IS IMPORTANT BECAUSE YOU GAIN A DEEPER UNDERSTANDING OF PEOPLE, THEIR JOURNEYS AND HOW YOUR ACTIONS MIGHT IMPACT THEM.

AN OPEN DOOR

Every single person in the world has been on a completely different journey. They've all had different upbringings and will all have different values and experiences. Part of being empathetic and open-minded means having curiosity rather than judgement. It's about understanding that someone might act, dress, speak or look a different way to you because of their own personal journey and background.

And even little things can impact the way someone behaves. You might not realize what's going on in their home lives, or how much sleep they had the night before. They might have had an argument with their parents, or have received some bad news. So having empathy and understanding that somebody could just be having a bad day is also really helpful to understanding others and building strong relationships.

When you're open, you're like an open door, inviting in knowledge, soaking things up like a sponge, considering different ways of thinking and alternative perspectives. When you're closed, you're like a shut door, so nothing and no one can get in. It's so much easier to connect with people if you are open!

LIONESSES' LESSONS

★ Could you join a team or a group if you're not already part of one? Your school might have clubs that you can join, or perhaps you live near a youth club. Or you could even set up a club yourself! Being part of a team has helped us develop our curiosity, openness and empathy because we always have to be thinking about other perspectives.

★ Boost your friends by celebrating their successes, and be there to help pick them back up when things don't go their way.

★ Next time you disagree with someone, try putting yourself in their 'football boots'. See things from their perspective before you respond. Stay curious.

★ Remember, we are all wired differently and have different opinions and expectations. If you always expect people to see or do things your way, you aren't being open to their thoughts and feelings.

★ Notice if any of your friends seem sad, low or angrier than usual. Let them know you care and that you are there, but you understand if they need space.

OUR SUPPORT SQUADS

Remember those Four Foundations of Friendship – enjoyment, trust, understanding and support? It's great to find a support squad who can give you all of these things – for now, it might be one person or two people who give you these things. Or maybe you're surrounded by lots of people who do! For us, as well as having each other, we each have people to confide in, people who make us laugh, someone to talk football with and someone to talk about everything but football with. These are the people who are closest to us, who we can turn to about anything, and who we feel the most at home with.

ELLA'S SUPPORT SQUAD

MUM and DAD

They got me where I am today and without them none of this would have been possible. They've always believed in me and pushed me to be the best I could be.

NAN

One of my best friends and my biggest fan! (She thinks she's famous now too, thanks to my YouTube videos.)

GAZ

My agent is like my second dad. Gaz believed in me when no one else did. I can trust him with everything and I know he'll do anything for me.

ABBIE McMANUS

My go-to person ever since she put her arm round me at Manchester City aged fourteen. She's like family, and no matter what, she'll always be there for me if I need her and vice versa. I'm lucky to have her.

JOE

My boyfriend, Joe, has been my rock since I met him. He gives me the best advice and understands my life and the sacrifices I have to make. He always wants the best for me.

THE GIRLS

(Lauren, Lauren, Ellie, Sheona and Morgan) This group of girls are like family to me. They've been my best friends since we were tiny and they'll be in my life forever.

LESS (ALESSIA RUSSO)

Alessia is like a sister and we've been on our football journey together since we were so young. We understand each other so well. I can trust Alessia with anything and know she will do everything to help me out when I need her.

GEORGIA'S SUPPORT SQUAD

LEAH WILLIAMSON

My England camp roomy since day one, Leah was my first and only ever roommate and is another of my besties.

KEIRA WALSH

I speak to Keira every day. We've known each other since Blackburn Rovers as teenagers and we moved to Manchester City, and have now both moved to play for European teams – Keira in Spain and me in Germany.

BAYERN BUDDIES

My Bayern teammates made my move to Germany so much easier by showing me lots of support and kindness.

MY FAMILY

I wouldn't be where I am today without their many hours of driving or their ongoing support and encouragement.

MENTOR

Luke is an incredible mentor who I meet with once a week.

STEPH HOUGHTON

Steph has always encouraged and challenged me to get the best out of myself. I'd like to think I bring out Steph's fun side in return!

DORON

Doron is my agent and one of the nicest people I've ever met – I can talk to him about anything. He brings out the best in me, and I don't ever want to let him down!

JILL SCOTT

The ultimate big sister – a great character to have in the dressing room, the most amazing and positive person you want around the team. She had so much trust and faith in my success, and would always remind me of that.

BETH

This is my friend who I can talk about everything *but* football with!

NIKITA'S SUPPORT SQUAD

KELSEY

My twin sister, Kelsey, is the first person I'll call to ask what she thinks, and to ask for her help if I need it.

FARA WILLIAMS, JILL SCOTT, DEMI STOKES and TONI DUGGAN

They genuinely care about me, and will pick up the phone whenever I call.

MUM

My mum and I are really close – we are friends as well as mum and daughter. I can always rely on my mum to be there for me.

WHO'S IN YOUR SUPPORT SQUAD?

Your squad might include your parents or caregivers, grandparents, siblings, friends, teachers or other trusted grown-ups. It doesn't matter if your support squad isn't filled with lots of people yet. You have plenty of time to meet people throughout your life who can provide you with all the enjoyment, trust, understanding and support you need.

Meanwhile, if you ever feel alone and like you don't have anyone to confide in, think about who else you could ask for help. There are lots of lovely kind people who volunteer their time to be on the end of a phone to help others. They, like us, know that you deserve to feel seen, heard and understood. So there really is someone there for everyone. (We've included a list of supportive organizations at the end of this book in case you ever need help. You can confide in them with confidence.)

★ FAMILY

Your squad might include your family or it might not. Families come in all different shapes and sizes. Some families are really close and do everything together. Others are more independent, where everyone does their own thing then comes back together from time to time. Some aren't close at all, and so people find their own extended family members in their friendships.

Nikita grew up with her mum, her twin sister and her two brothers, but would still go and watch her dad play football. Her mum worked multiple jobs, and when she came home after work she created a loving family environment. She'd insist they ate meals as a family, and they had games night on Saturdays, and post-match Sunday roasts. Georgia's parents split up when she was little and she became quite independent, while Ella's mum and dad are still together, and she has a very close relationship with her nan.

We've all got different family units and different relationships within them, and we understand that not everyone has that support system.

❝ LUCKILY, FRIENDS ARE THE FAMILY YOU CHOOSE FOR YOURSELF. ❞

★ FRIENDS

Some people have a large group of friends, and some just a few small groups. Other people have just one or two close friends. There is no right or wrong, but remember that QUALITY matters more than QUANTITY. It's much better to have a small number of good-quality relationships than lots of poor-quality ones that don't make you feel happy, loved or supported.

★ PICKING YOUR SQUAD

Now it's your turn! Grab a piece of paper and draw a picture of yourself, like the ones of us on pages 189–192. Now have a think about the people you are close to, who provide those all-important things – enjoyment, trust, understanding and support. These are the things you could think about:

★ Who can you confide in?

★ Who makes you laugh?

★ Who has similar values to you?

★ Who shows an interest and listens to you?

★ Who celebrates your successes and supports you when you're feeling low?

★ Who are your encouragers and challengers who bring the best out of you?

★ Who sticks up for you and has your back?

★ Who makes you feel comfortable?

★ Who makes you feel happy?

Now add labels to your self-portrait and write the names of all the people who come to mind. Perhaps there is a small handful of names or perhaps you need a second piece of paper as there are so many people! Either way, hopefully your list contains at least one or two people who provide you with love, friendship, laughter and support. Remember, you have plenty of time throughout your life to find people to build these kinds of friendships with. You don't need to have a full squad now!

V.I.P.

There is another V.I.P. (Very Important Person) who should be in your support squad. Do you know who that is? It's YOU!

IT'S IMPORTANT TO BE YOUR OWN BEST FRIEND, AND SOMETIMES YOU NEED TIME TO YOURSELF TO BUILD THAT CONNECTION.

Having some 'me time' gives you space to think. It's important to have that space, and to learn to enjoy your own company as you grow up and start to become more independent. And time alone can be soothing, especially when you're constantly surrounded by other people. When you do have alone time, please try to be kind to yourself and treat yourself like you would your own best friend.

We've spent this chapter explaining how to be kind to friends, and you must always remember to also apply these lessons to how you treat yourself. Be kind to yourself, say positive things, celebrate when things go well and listen to your body if you're feeling tired or sad or angry or low. Support yourself as much as you would support your best mates.

MAKING NEW FRIENDS

You're probably at a time in your life when you're meeting new people all the time, whether you're joining new clubs or teams, or have recently started or are due to start a new school. You're going to come across so many people in your life, and it might be that you want to befriend them!

But it isn't always easy to know what to say to people you don't know. Sometimes it feels much more comfortable to just stay quiet and not say anything at all. It's difficult, the first few times, to pluck up the courage to start a conversation, but once you do, the hardest bit is over and done with. And, once you've done it a few times and you see it wasn't as bad as you thought (because it never is), you'll soon realize it's always worth a try! The worst that can happen is that they have nothing to say, and then you can just shrug and move on.

There are some obvious questions you can ask to get to know someone new, such as 'Hi, how are you?', or you could compliment what they're wearing – for example, 'I like your trainers.' (That was the first thing Tooney said to Alessia Russo when they met as they had the same trainers on, just in different colours.) But you can probably do better than that! Here are a few ideas for conversation-starters with people you don't know:

★ Try 'would you rather' questions to spark the conversation. For example: 'If you had to choose superpowers, would you rather be invisible or be able to fly?' Ask them why and then share which you'd rather have. Are there any other 'would you rather' questions that you can think of?

★ Ask them:

 ☆ 'What's the best thing that's happened this week?'

 ☆ 'Who would your dream football team be and why?'

 ☆ 'What's your favourite TV show/film/musical?'

 ☆ 'What football team do you support and who's your favourite player?'

 ☆ 'If you could go anywhere in the world right now – to any country – where would you go?'

WITH QUESTIONS LIKE THESE, YOU MIGHT FIND YOURSELF BONDING AND MAKING FRIENDS WITH PEOPLE YOU NEVER THOUGHT YOU WOULD!

Building your own support squad is one of the best things you can do for your wellbeing, no matter how big or small the squad is. Life is full of ups and downs, and your support squad can help you to navigate through the twists and turns along the way and give you a soft place to land when things feel hard. There can be times when things are tough and it's important to have people who are there for you, like you are for them. That's squad goals.

'NOW GO OUT THERE, LIKE A TRUE LIONESS, AND ROAR WITH THE REST OF YOUR PRIDE!'

CHAPTER FIVE: TAKING AIM AT WHAT MATTERS MOST

ELLA

All eyes were on the ball, waiting to see if it would cross the line and hit the back of the net. It felt like forever before it actually did, like time was in slow motion, from when it left my boot until it went over German goalkeeper Merle Frohms's head. I'd never felt it before: a feeling of urgency where all I could think was, 'Why is it taking so long?!' Finally, when everyone started screaming, I knew it was real. The ball had actually gone in. I'd just scored a goal at Wembley in the European Cup final!

That's when the whole stadium of over 87,000 fans erupted. It was literally the best feeling of my life!

I've got footage of that goal saved on my phone and I watch it sometimes before bed, just to relive it. It was such a pinch-me moment, one that will stay with me forever. In the clip you see Keira Walsh looking up and seeing me making a run, pointing. Keira always knows where I am on the pitch, she's unbelievable in midfield, and rightly earned Player of the Game in that match. The video shows her play a perfect pass in to me. Then the keeper came out, and I chipped the ball over her.

It was a tense match, which ended up going to extra time when Germany scored an equalizer. But Chloe Kelly scored in the 110th minute, and, when the final whistle blew, I ran towards Alessia Russo and jumped into her arms, tears streaming down my face. We'd done it! We'd just won the Euros!

THE QUEEN EVEN SENT A STATEMENT TO US, SAYING: 'YOUR SUCCESS GOES FAR BEYOND THE TROPHY YOU HAVE SO DESERVEDLY EARNED. YOU HAVE ALL SET AN EXAMPLE THAT WILL BE AN INSPIRATION FOR GIRLS AND WOMEN TODAY, AND FOR FUTURE GENERATIONS.'

After this came a LOT of dancing around the stadium, singing in the changing rooms, and if you look on YouTube you can see clips of us gatecrashing the press conference and chanting, 'It's coming home' in front of all the journalists. I didn't sleep at all that night!

Time stood still during that slo-mo goal moment, but it raced from the final whistle until we went home. It was mad, and that's the funny thing about time — you can lose all track of it when you're fully immersed in what you're doing.

WHY WE PLAY

Scoring that goal and winning that championship meant achieving the ultimate success, the motivation that drives all professional athletes — to win. But success is only one reason why we play football.

There are loads of other reasons why we play it. Firstly, we play because we enjoy it, because it's our spark (more on that later!). We also play to make our families proud — seeing them in the stands at our matches feels amazing. We play to prove to ourselves that we can achieve whatever we put our minds to when we give it our all.

But, more than that, and as the queen said, we play football to inspire future generations and to make a difference. And that's what these next two chapters are all about.

ENGAGEMENT: DOING SOMETHING YOU ENJOY SO MUCH THAT YOU GET THE MAXIMUM POSSIBLE ENJOYMENT FROM IT, AND POSSIBLY EVEN LOSE TRACK OF TIME.

MEANING: HAVING A STRONG ENOUGH 'WHY' (OR PURPOSE) BEHIND WHAT YOU DO TO MAKE IT MEANINGFUL.

Remember that 'Engagement' and 'Meaning' are two of the six pillars of wellbeing that we talked about in the introduction to this book. These pillars contribute to our mental health and wellness. Here's a reminder of them all: PERMA-V stands for Positive Emotion, Engagement, Relationships, Meaning, Accomplishment and Vitality.

Let's start with engagement – what exactly is it and why is it good for our mental health?

FINDING FLOW

Can you think of a time when you've been so absorbed by what you're doing that you lost track of time? This maximum level of engagement is called 'flow' – a concept coined by psychologist Mihaly Csikszentmihalyi. It's when you are so involved in what you're doing that you don't get those random thoughts that pop into our heads, like, 'I wonder what will happen if I . . .' or, 'I mustn't forget to do . . .' When you're enjoying something in this way, you're not really thinking about anything else, you're just 'in the zone'.

That's what playing football feels like for me. It's freedom from all that mind chatter we all have going on in our heads sometimes. Finding my flow in football allows me to be properly present in the moment, rather than worrying about the past or the future.

Many of us have a tendency to spend too much time fixating on things that have already happened or worrying about what's going to happen next, rather than on the here and now. We all have to remind ourselves sometimes to be present and to pay attention to exactly what's happening around us. Doing this helps us make the most of each fleeting moment. The added bonus is, when you savour a moment while it's actually happening, you don't just enjoy it more there and then, but it makes it easier to relive that moment later on as well, as you've committed it to memory.

THE FLOW ZONE

You already have some tools in your kitbag to help you with being more present – savouring moments and practising mindfulness and taking time to feel gratitude for what you have. Finding activities that get you in the flow zone is another good tactic for staying present.

But how do you ramp up your level of engagement, to get into the flow zone and quieten all that mind chatter? Well, it's all about finding the right kind of activities. These are usually things that:

★ you can concentrate on;

★ you can set clear goals for;

★ you can get feedback about how well you're doing;

★ are challenging enough to engage you, but not so difficult that goals aren't achievable;

★ you have control over.

Of course, if you ask us what activity we would suggest, it would definitely be sport! You don't have to play football – there's hockey, netball, athletics, table tennis, cricket, golf, running and so much more! But if you're not keen on sport, you could find something else that you love. Here are some other examples of activities that might help you get into the flow zone and enjoy yourself to the max:

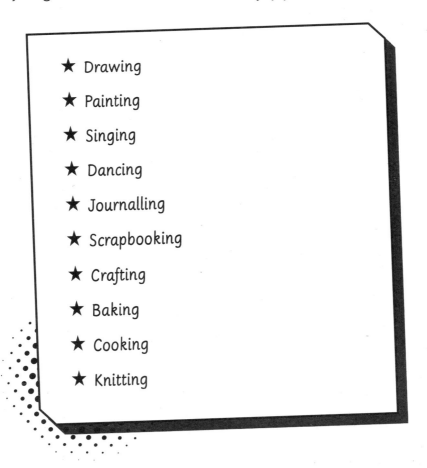

★ Drawing

★ Painting

★ Singing

★ Dancing

★ Journalling

★ Scrapbooking

★ Crafting

★ Baking

★ Cooking

★ Knitting

And so much more! Is there an activity that you would add to this list?

FINDING YOUR SPARK

Your spark is whatever lights you up when you do it. It's the thing that ignites the flame to make you want to do well. It's something that fascinates you, which you really enjoy doing. There's no right or wrong time to uncover your spark. Some people find it when they're very young and some don't find it until they're older. But we want to help you find your spark, so you can enjoy it for as long as possible!

Experts say that when children and teenagers know their spark and have people around them who support it, they're more likely to be physically and mentally healthy, to have a sense of purpose, to be better at helping others, and even to do well in education. So, what they're saying is, if we find something we *love* to do, it can make us happier, kinder and better at school? Um, yes, please!

❝ HAVING A SPARK CAN HELP YOU FEEL GOOD ABOUT YOURSELF. AND THAT'S WHAT THE THREE OF US WANT FOR YOU. ❞

SO, WHAT EXACTLY IS A 'SPARK'?

Dr Peter Benson was a psychologist and author who devoted his life to studying how young people develop. He said that sparks fall into one of the following categories:

★ Something you're good at – this could be anything, such as playing football, a musical instrument, drawing or making things with your hands, and more.

★ Something you care about – such as animals, nature or helping other people.

★ A special characteristic – such as being a good friend, listener or kind person.

WHY FOOTBALL?

Before we help you find your spark and talk about the different ways that you can ignite it, and keep it lit, can you guess what our spark is? Of course you can! It's football! But why does football light each of us up?

All three of us have always been active people. Growing up, Keets loved racing around on her bike, G played cricket, netball and football at county level, and I loved getting stuck into every single sport I could.

There was something about football in particular, though, that made my eyes sparkle and made me feel alive. Football was just different. I absolutely loved it (and I was good at it, which helped!). But I think what I liked the most was being part of a team environment, and being totally absorbed in what was happening on the pitch. When I played football, I would lose track of time because I was so focused on the game. I could just forget about anything else and get into this zone where nothing else mattered – only the next pass.

To this day, when I step out on to the pitch, I don't think about what time it is, what day it is, what I'm going to do after the match, or anything else. I'm just focused on playing football and getting better.

For Keets, it's the feeling of competing that sparks her and keeps her motivated. It's not scoring goals, but the *challenge* of getting past the defender and beating the goalkeeper.

For G, it's the safety of the team environment that makes football her spark. She felt much more nervous competing as an individual in athletics.

QUIZ: WHAT'S YOUR SPARK?

IT'S YOUR TURN NOW! LET'S FIND OUT WHAT LIGHTS YOU UP. READY?

★ Is there an activity you do where you get so engaged in what you're doing that you can totally lose track of time? Is it a sport? Is it being outdoors in nature? Or a creative activity? Is it spending time alone and writing? Or reading a good book? Or cooking up a feast?

★ Is there an activity you do that makes you feel safe and like you belong? An activity where you feel like you're a part of something? It could be acting in a play, or singing in a band, or playing sport for a team.

★ Is there an activity that challenges you – and where you enjoy that challenge? It could be chess or rock climbing or trying to beat your personal best on a run.

★ What do you care about? Are there any issues that you feel particularly strongly about? Or something or someone that you care about deeply? Perhaps it's animals, or your friends, or the climate, or women's rights (for example, we care a LOT about making sure young girls have the choice to play football, and we're all very motivated by this).

★ What are you good at? Remember, you can still be very good at something without having medals and trophies to prove it. Are you a good team player? Is there a game you always win? Think outside the box – everyone has different skills and that's what makes the world so interesting!

★ What would your friends and family say you are good at? What words might they use to describe your best qualities? (Maybe it's creative, thoughtful, funny?) Why not ask them directly, if you're not sure!

★ What do you do when you're bored? (Not including reaching for a phone or electronic device.) Boredom can be a great way to find your spark. When you haven't got anything to do, you have to make your own fun. You might draw, sing, read, design, construct, dance. Anything at all!

★ What makes you happy and gives you energy when you do it? It might help to start by thinking of activities that give you the opposite feeling! So is there a subject at school that you find boring and makes you feel tired? Or a game that your friends like that you just can't seem to get into? Now you can rule these things out, have a think about what lifts you up and has the opposite effect entirely. What do you look forward to doing?

Hopefully by now, you have an idea of a few things:

★ an activity, subject, task or thing you LOVE to do

★ something you care a LOT about

★ what you're GOOD at.

Once you know what your spark is, you can fan the flames and keep the spark alive by finding ways to do what you love more often.

Think about:

★ Are there any groups or people or teams who share similar passions and values? Could you join them or spend more time with them?

★ Are there any books you could read that will help you master your spark? Can you find videos or tutorials on YouTube to help you practise?

★ Is there a way to spread the word about a cause you care about?

★ Could you make a promise to yourself to spend time on your spark – maybe at least once a week? Devoting time to your spark will make you feel good, and it'll help you to grow and get better at it too.

GEORGIA

When both your parents are PE teachers, like mine, it's kind of expected that you're going to end up doing something sporty. Growing up, I played netball, cricket, football, table tennis – and that's not even half of it!

Recently, the FC Bayern Munich girls and I decided to play a game of golf. Most of the girls were struggling to hold the club correctly because they hadn't played before, but there I was hitting the ball pretty far. They were bemused and thought it must just be beginner's luck. I eventually owned up and explained that I'd had golf lessons as a kid. In fact, I'm really pleased I tried so many different sports and other activities when I was growing up – it's what helped me find my spark.

When I was twelve years old, I stopped playing football for a while because I was no longer allowed to play in the boys' team. The only local girls' team didn't play matches in a league, they just trained. So I focused on playing lots of other sports instead and although I enjoyed them, it felt like something was missing. Obviously, it was football. That's when I knew for certain that football was my spark.

As soon as I realized how much I missed it, I was out on the field behind our house, kicking a ball about once again. But it took me a year to persuade my mum to take me to the trial at Blackburn Rovers, which was a long drive away.

ALL THAT PERSUADING (BY ME) AND DRIVING (BY MY MUM) PAID OFF EVENTUALLY THOUGH – I BECAME THE TOP GOAL SCORER AND WAS SIGNED TO MANCHESTER CITY SOON AFTERWARDS, KICK-STARTING MY PROFESSIONAL CAREER. THAT SPARK IGNITED A FLAME!

GEORGIA'S GREAT GUIDE TO IGNITING YOUR SPARK

★ Get stuck in. It's good to try lots of different things to find what you truly enjoy. In the process of trying a variety of activities, you may notice which ones you miss the most if you stop doing them.

★ You don't have to stop trying new activities once you find your spark – if you happen to find there are lots of things you enjoy, then that's great!

★ It doesn't matter if you haven't found your spark yet. The more you try, the more likely you are to find it.

★ Even if something isn't your 'spark', if you're enjoying it and it's good for you then keep going. It might turn into a spark over time, because with practice things become easier and possibly even more fun!

TURN OFF, SWITCH ON

You, like the three of us, are part of the 'digital native' generation. This means that since we were all very young children, we have been surrounded by technology and have never known a time without the internet, smartphones and other devices. As we said in chapter three, there are so many great things about having technology at our fingertips – from communicating with friends and family to having a whole wealth of information just a few clicks away. But it also means that it's far too easy to become plugged-in and tuned-out.

When you have a phone of your own (if you haven't already got one), you might find yourself looking down at the screen regularly. You might also find your parents nag you to put it down a lot!

Look, we could go on for hours debating the good and bad things about phones (perhaps we'll save that for another book!). But the point is, if you have your head down in your phone all day, you'll never have time to explore different activities and find the ones that you love.

> IT'S DURING MOMENTS OF DOWNTIME THAT YOU COULD FIND SOMETHING THAT REALLY SPARKS YOUR INTEREST.

THE VALUE OF VALUES

We've talked a lot about which activities you enjoy, but before we finish this chapter, I want you to spend a bit of time thinking about what bothers you. I know that sounds weird, but this is a tactic that can help you to uncover your values and what matters most to you.

For instance, dishonesty is something Keets can't stand, unfairness really frustrates Tooney, and it annoys me when people are closed off to different opinions or ideas. One thing that bothers all of us is inequality – whether that's gender inequality or racial inequality or any other kind of inequality. We strongly feel that everyone should be treated the same and have the same opportunities to do what they love and be who they are.

So how about you? Is there something that makes you feel frustrated or bothered? It might be when people drop litter and show disregard for the environment, or when someone is cruel to an animal or a person, or when somebody cheats in a game or tells a lie?

Thinking about what bothers us is helpful because those things point like signposts to what we truly care about, what matters most to us, and what we value. And strong or shared values can bring people together to make positive change, as we'll talk more about in the next chapter.

Our team of Lionesses are so passionate about making the world a better place. Each of us has different issues that we campaign for and, outside of football, fighting for a fairer world is a spark for many of us. Here are some of the causes we've been shouting about:

★ Gender inequality: when girls and boys are treated differently – for example, boys being able to play football in PE and girls not being given that option.

★ Raising awareness about Prader-Willi syndrome (PWS), a cause close to Ella's heart because her cousin's daughter, Nellie, has the condition.

★ When people of different backgrounds, races, ethnicities and religions are treated unfairly.

★ Bullying: when people say mean things to others and treat them unkindly.

Getting to know your own values and the causes that you care about is another way to find your spark. So, if you're someone who values animal rights, your spark might be found in campaigning for fair treatment of animals. Or if you are someone who really values women's rights, perhaps you can join us in our fight to make sure all girls can play football!

We hope this chapter has helped you on your journey to discovering your spark, and what matters most to you. The better we know the things we enjoy, the things we're good at and the things we value, the more time we can spend engaged in these things. This can help us to bring more joy and meaning into our lives, and to go after our dreams. Plus, the better we know ourselves, the easier it is to find those who share our values, join forces and work together towards a common goal.

CHAPTER SIX:
THE POWER OF PURPOSE

ELLA

The 2022 Women's Euros was record-breaking in loads of ways.

★ It had the highest attendance of any Euros final, with 87,192 people coming along to watch us. (Before that, the record crowd attendance was 79,115 for the men's Euros final of Spain vs Soviet Union back in 1964!)

★ Our amazing coach, Sarina Wiegman, was the first coach to win the European Championship with two different nations (England in 2022 and Netherlands in 2017).

★ The Lionesses broke Germany's goal-scoring record, by scoring twenty-two across the tournament.

DID YOU KNOW THAT SEVEN OF THOSE TWENTY-TWO GOALS WERE SCORED BY SUBSTITUTES? WHEN SUBS CAME OFF THE BENCH WE HAD ONE CLEAR PURPOSE–TO HAVE AN IMPACT ON THE GAME AND MAKE A DIFFERENCE. AND THAT'S EXACTLY WHAT WE DID!

Purpose is basically about the impact you want to have. It's doing something based on a strong reason behind it. For us, our purpose was to positively impact the game. Why? Because we wanted to win the championship and take home the trophy.

When Alessia Russo came on as a sub in the games against Sweden, Northern Ireland and Norway, she scored each time. And in the final game – the important match against Germany that would decide who would win the whole tournament – I came off the bench in the 56th minute. The score was 0–0 when I came on, and six minutes later I chipped the ball into the back of the net to put us 1–0 up.

When the German midfielder Lina Magull scored the equalizer in the 79th minute, we were forced into extra time. That's when Sarina made her third substitution, bringing Chloe Kelly on. In the 110th minute, Chloe scored and we went on to win the tournament! So, both goals for England in the final were scored by substitutes.

Whether we were in the starting line-up, or brought on halfway through the game, or during the final minutes, Sarina made us all feel valued. She made it clear that every single one of us had an important role to play, a clear purpose. We knew that when we came on, we had to change the game.

❝ THIS STRONG SENSE OF PURPOSE WAS ONE OF THE REASONS WE WON THE EUROS! ❞

FINDING YOUR PURPOSE

When I'm on the pitch, I'm always motivated by the purpose to make an impact. So, while my *dream* has always been to be a professional footballer, my *purpose* is to make an impact on each game I play and to inspire the next generation. Do you see the difference? Having a purpose means I'm doing what I do for a reason that means a lot to me.

In chapter two we spoke about identifying your superpowers. It's time to think back to this, and remember what you said your skills and strengths are. We're going to use this to help you find your purpose!

Let me show you some examples about myself . . .

ON THE PITCH

★ My SUPERPOWER: getting on the ball, turning quickly, finding pockets of space.

★ My PURPOSE: making an impact on the game to help us win.

IN LIFE

★ My SUPERPOWER: being hardworking, driven and focused on my dream to succeed as a footballer.

★ My PURPOSE: being a positive role model and helping young girls realize they can also achieve their dreams.

I want you to think about your purpose now. Consider an intention or motivation you have when you play your favourite sport with a team, or take part in a hobby on your own, or work on something at school or at home. Grab a pen and paper and fill in the gaps:

I AM REALLY GOOD AT ...

AND I DO ...

BECAUSE ...

Perhaps you're really good at sprinting, and you do relay races because it helps you feel fit and healthy?

Or perhaps you're good at art and love drawing so you regularly make birthday cards for friends and family because your parents and carers are busy and it saves them having to buy cards all the time?

Or maybe you get good grades at school, and you stay on top of your homework because you want to feel proud of your achievements in all your subjects.

> KNOWING YOUR PURPOSE MAKES THE THINGS YOU DO MEANINGFUL. AND HAVING MEANING IN YOUR LIFE IS IMPORTANT FOR YOUR HAPPINESS AND WELLBEING.

I never imagined, when I first started playing, that I would see young girls with my name on the backs of their football shirts. Or that I would get to join forces with England footballer Phil Foden along with Football Beyond Borders charity and Nike to open a community football pitch in Moss Side, Manchester. I'm so proud as a female footballer to have got to where I am now, and it feels really special to be in this position. My purpose – to be a good role model – motivates me to keep going. And there's no greater feeling than hearing from young fans that they've been inspired by the Lionesses to dream big and go after their goals.

For me, that's the most meaningful thing in the world.

TOONEY'S TOP TIPS ON STEPPING INTO YOUR POWER WITH PURPOSE

★ Remember your UNIQUE superpowers.

★ Think about HOW you use them (or how you can start to, if you don't use them already).

★ Then, be aware of WHY you use them – your purpose, reason or motivation.

★ When life throws you a curveball, don't forget your purpose. It will help you get back up when you've been knocked down.

GEORGIA

A TEAM WITH DREAMS

'Play for the little girl who dreamed of being where you are now,' Sarina Wiegman once said to the England squad. I looked around at my teammates and thought about how we've all been on such different journeys to get to where we are today. That's why what Sarina said really hit home. It reminded me that I was there with each of these other little-girls-all-grown-up for a reason.

Each one of us had missed out on some normal parts of our childhoods to pursue our dreams. All that time and money invested. Moving away from home at sixteen. Missing birthdays and other important events in family and friends' lives. I don't see it as a sacrifice, as I obviously chose to devote so much of my life to football. It was all done in order to reach my goal of being here right now, playing for my country. I play for that little girl with a big dream – and in that moment it all felt worth it.

" WE EACH PLAY FOR OUR YOUNGER SELVES, WHO DREAMED OF BEING WHERE WE ARE NOW, AND ALSO FOR THE YOUNG GIRLS TODAY WHO WANT TO FOLLOW IN OUR FOOTSTEPS. "

As Tooney just explained, finding your purpose is important, because it guides you forward, gives you meaning and helps you feel good and fulfilled.

And there's an added bonus too. When you have a strong WHY, or a clear purpose for doing things, it makes it easier to withstand the bumps in the road, to cope with knockbacks and face challenges head-on. Purpose gives you the grit and drive and power to go again, because your mind is focused on *why* you chose to do something in the first place.

There are lots of knocks and challenges to deal with in football, and there's a lot of pressure. The highs are very high – so you feel on top of the world when you get selected to play for your country, win a trophy, score a goal for your team or win a match. But the lows can be difficult to deal with: the rejection of not being selected, the injuries, the losses. But with a strong meaningful purpose guiding you forward – a WHY for doing what you do – the lows become easier to cope with. So, when I focus on the fact that I'm playing for younger-Georgia and young girls everywhere, this keeps me going when times get tough.

Say you didn't get picked to be in the school play, for example, but your 'WHY' for acting and auditioning is to help you feel more confident and make friends. You know that it's important to you to achieve these two things, and keeping these purposes in mind can motivate you to audition again for the next play, and not feel too defeated this time.

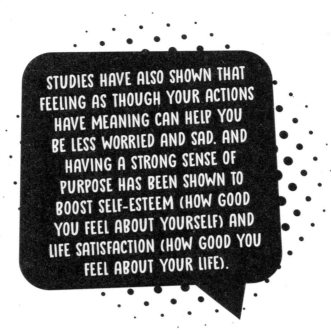

STUDIES HAVE ALSO SHOWN THAT FEELING AS THOUGH YOUR ACTIONS HAVE MEANING CAN HELP YOU BE LESS WORRIED AND SAD. AND HAVING A STRONG SENSE OF PURPOSE HAS BEEN SHOWN TO BOOST SELF-ESTEEM (HOW GOOD YOU FEEL ABOUT YOURSELF) AND LIFE SATISFACTION (HOW GOOD YOU FEEL ABOUT YOUR LIFE).

This is why we want you to find YOUR purpose. We want to help you find meaning and live your best life. It doesn't matter whether your purpose is to succeed and excel at whatever you do, or champion a cause that matters to you – it's just about having that reason to keep you going.

And if you aren't sure what your WHY is just yet, don't worry. Perhaps you could help us on our mission to make football a sport that can be enjoyed by EVERYONE? I'll let Nikita tell you more about that . . .

NIKITA

After the Euros, in September 2022, as I stood, surrounded by young people from my home community in Toxteth, unveiling a plaque that read *'Nikita Parris – Puma Sports Court'*, I couldn't have felt happier. Puma had agreed to sponsor my idea of refurbishing the sports court at the youth centre where I started my football journey. These courts had been well used and were in need of some care.

This community had given me so much growing up, and the youth centre was my safe space where my dream of becoming a footballer began. Even if the computers or table-tennis bats were broken or the balls were missing from the pool table, all we needed was a football and two goals, and we could spend hours playing. So, helping to improve this safe place for a new generation of children in the area felt like everything had come full circle. Underneath my name on the plaque, it said: *'Nikita Parris and Puma have built this court to inspire the youth of Toxteth to play sports and chase their dreams.'*

To be able to make an actual difference to the lives of young people who live in this community means so much to me. I think that's what I've always wanted to do deep down – to 'be the change'. Whether that's in a game of football, in a classroom, or in my neighbourhood, my purpose has always been to **make a difference** somehow, to support others.

I had another opportunity to do that when, in September 2018, I launched the NP17 Academy at the City of Liverpool College to sponsor fourteen girls aged seventeen to nineteen through a full-time educational qualification. Education has always been important to me so the purpose of this partnership with the university was to provide opportunities for talented female footballers from deprived areas of Liverpool to further their education and discover the many different options for careers in sport. The NP17 Academy ran successfully for a few years until the Covid-19 pandemic hit, and I loved being able to support young women from the local community in a meaningful way.

There are so many caring people out there who are keen to make a difference by supporting others. Earl Jenkins started Kingsley United over twenty years ago to keep kids in Toxteth off the streets and on the pitches. But what he's done reaches further than that. His devotion and support kick-started my own football journey and now that little girl he once coached is doing her best to inspire others just starting out on theirs. His purposeful actions had a ripple effect. Now, that's powerful!

"YOU NEVER REALLY KNOW THE POSITIVE IMPACT YOU'RE GOING TO HAVE ON PEOPLE."

I've found that having a purpose gives you a real sense of your own power and potential to make an actual difference, whether that's to your own life or to other people's lives. And you certainly don't need to change the entire world to make a difference. It all counts. Sometimes there's a lot of pressure on young people to fix all these big problems that grown-ups made in the first place. But these problems, like gender inequality and climate change, can feel massive and it's difficult to know where to start! We'll go on to some of these larger issues soon, but if you're not sure where to begin, the best thing to do is start small! Here are some examples of small actions that can make positive changes:

★ Say something kind to someone.

★ Help a friend or sibling or family member with something they're struggling with.

★ Pick up litter.

★ Be supportive. Speak up as an ally for anyone being treated unfairly.

★ Volunteer your time at school or for a local club.

★ Visit a care home and sing or play an instrument for the residents, or simply stay and chat to them.

'REMEMBER, ANY CONTRIBUTION IS WORTHWHILE, NO MATTER HOW SMALL.'

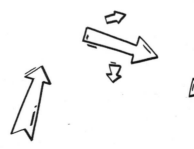

USE YOUR MAGIC WAND

If we had a magic wand, all three of us would want to create an equal world where everyone has the same access to opportunities and resources, and where we are all treated the same.

At the moment, there's not enough diversity in the top levels of women's football. One reason for this is that people of colour don't always have the same access to the opportunities that can help them get on the ladder in the first place.

For me, part of my purpose is to create equal access for everyone who might want to play football. For example, most of the coaching centres and clubs that are part of the pathway towards becoming a Lioness tend to be in areas in the suburbs, which are not easy to get to if you live in inner-city areas. But many people of colour and families from disadvantaged backgrounds live in inner-city areas, which means these children can't get to these clubs! If they don't have a parent or family member who can drive them there and back, they need to travel by public transport on their own (often in the evenings, after dark). But this could be dangerous and lots of parents don't want their children doing this. So most young people from cities aren't given an equal chance of playing at an elite level. This is why many teams end up with players who are often white and all from similar, more privileged backgrounds.

We need to remove barriers like this if we want football to be for everyone! For example, we need more academies to be built in inner-city areas. And we need more local-council funding for safe transport, such as mini-buses, to take children to and from elite training facilities.

This would make professional football a more accessible pathway for everyone, and should improve the chances of people from all backgrounds being represented in top league teams.

WHAT WOULD YOU FIX IF YOU HAD A MAGIC WAND?

FIGHT FOR **YOUR** RIGHTS

Remember at the start of this book we mentioned that in 1921, women's football was banned because it was deemed an 'unsuitable' sport for women? And that this ban stuck around for fifty years before it was finally lifted in 1971? Well, up until very recently, female England and Women's Super League players needed to work second jobs as they weren't being paid enough to make a living. This is still the case in other leagues, but female footballers in the WSL can now earn a respectable salary and attract sponsorship deals without having to find a second job.

One country that has fought hard for equality in football is America. In the USA, the women's national team (USWNT) is ranked number one in the world and is more successful than the men's national team (MNT), and has been totally outperforming them for a whole generation. For example, at the time of writing, the US women have won four World Cups since the team first formed in 1985, while the men haven't reached a semi-final since 1930! The USWNT bring in more interest and more money too. More people watch the women's game than watch the men's, and they sell more tickets and merchandise.

Despite that, until 2022, the female players were paid less than the men and earned less prize money. They've fought for many years for equal treatment and equal pay, and in 2022 their efforts paid off. They reached an agreement where the prize money earned by each team will be shared with the other, and shares of ticket sales and bonuses will also be equal. As USWNT legend and leader of the fight for equal pay, Megan Rapinoe, said, 'When we win, everyone wins.'

There's still a big difference in the prize money awarded by FIFA for male and female tournaments. In fact, men's teams earn more for a *loss* in a World Cup qualifying game than women earn for winning the whole tournament! But the women's World Cup prize money total has been raised in 2023, and male and female players are now paid the same to represent England, so we are moving in the right direction.

AND IF MORE AND MORE PEOPLE GET BEHIND WOMEN'S TEAMS AND COME TO WATCH OUR GAMES, WE CAN CONTINUE TO GROW AND CLOSE THAT GAP!

We have proven that women can play professional football with a level of grit and skill that captures the hearts of the nation. And that women *can* win a major championship, something that hadn't been done by any English team, male or female, for fifty-six years.

For us, equality in sport is about recognizing that the men's and women's games deserve equal opportunities, equal resources and equal respect. If we can continue to increase  interest in the women's game so that more people come to watch matches and buy merchandise, we can close the pay gap too. Being part of this conversation and speaking up for equality gives our lives so much meaning. And seeing the women's game growing and people's attitudes towards it shifting makes us so proud.

And we've been doing everything we can to make sure that football is available to everyone of ALL ages. After the Euros, we discovered some shocking stats. According to the Football Association, in the UK in 2022, just 63% of girls were offered football in PE lessons (72% in primary and just 44% in secondary schools) compared to 100% of boys being offered football in PE. Also, only 46% of schools give girls the same extracurricular opportunities in after-school sports clubs that they give to boys.

We all wanted this to change. Led by our Lioness teammate Lotte Wubben-Moy and captain, Leah Williamson, we wrote a letter to the UK government about how important it is for both girls and boys to have an equal opportunity to be involved in sport at school, and to give *everyone* access to football.

WE WROTE: 'This is an opportunity to make a huge difference. A change that will impact millions of young girls' lives. We ask you to make it a priority to invest in girls' football in schools, so that every girl has the choice.' We also asked that 'all girls have access to a minimum of two hours a week in PE'.

AND THE GOVERNMENT AGREED! THE PRIME MINISTER SAID: 'Last year the Lionesses' victory changed the game. Young girls know when they take to the pitch that football is for them and, thanks to the Lionesses, they too could be a part of the next generation to bring it home for their country. We want schools to build on this legacy.'

The government now requires schools in England to offer equal access to football and sports, plus a minimum of two hours of PE per week. And they are supplying additional funding to give girls equal opportunities to do sports at school.

This is a massive step forward. We gave a big Lioness roar, as loud as we could, to create change that will live on for years to come. And this made our win more meaningful than any of us could have thought possible.

NIKITA'S NIFTY NOTES ON MAKING A DIFFERENCE

You too can make a difference and create a legacy!

★ Brainstorm what you'd like to change or improve in your local area or at your school. Then choose a relevant activity that you can do to help the cause. For example, if you're passionate about the environment, you could join a tree-planting scheme (the Woodland Trust give away free packs of trees to schools and communities). Or if you want to help keep local kids safe, you could help paint and decorate a local community hub or speak to your local youth centre and see if there are other ways you could volunteer your time to help them. Or if you want to help those in need, you could ask for donations of coats, shoes, clothing or even football boots to give to those who need them. (See the Useful Resources on pages 337–339 for more ways to help.)

★ Do something challenging to raise money for your cause. You could do a sponsored walk, run, keepy-uppy challenge, game of netball, silence or anything else that you can think of!

★ Collaborate. Join forces with others to make an even bigger difference, like I did with Puma and Ella did with Nike. You could contact companies who might share your purpose and want to do something for the local community that helps them achieve their mission too.

★ Write a letter to your local MP asking for their help with raising awareness and improving your cause.

★ Start a petition to encourage other people to support your cause.

★ Remember what matters most to you and wear those values on your sleeve with pride, like the captain's band in a game of football! At the end of the day or week, ask yourself whether you've lived by your values and what you could do tomorrow or next week to live by them even more.

★ Be kind and treat everyone the same – no matter who they are and what their background is. Always treat people how you'd wish to be treated – the world needs more kindness and respect.

Having a clear purpose can make you a kinder, happier person – and make the world a better place too. Your purpose acts as a kind of compass, showing you what direction to go in. And it keeps you moving when you encounter bumps in the road or stormy weather along the way. We've found our 'WHY' through football and through fighting (and roaring!) for equal rights for girls and women. We hope we've got you one step closer to finding yours and stepping into your power too!

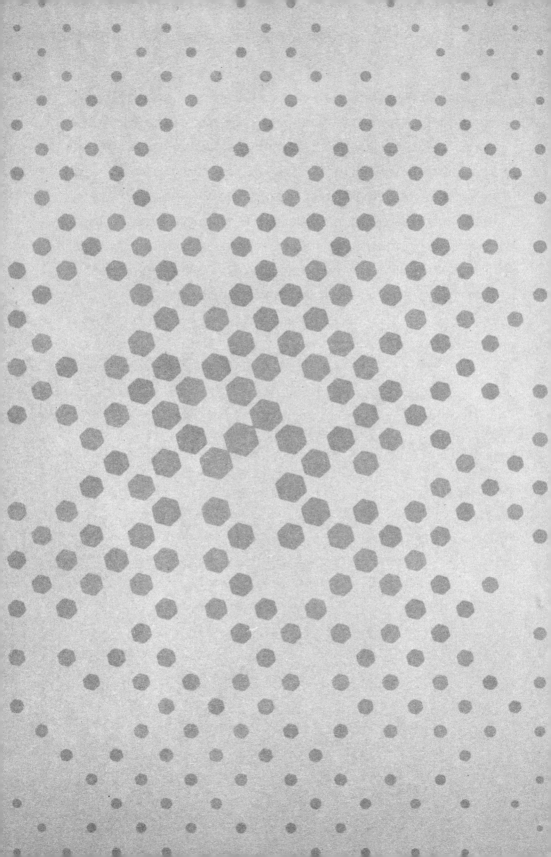

PART THREE
SHE SCORES

CHAPTER SEVEN: GOAL!

ELLA

LITTLE GIRL, BIG DREAM

When I was eight years old, my academy teammates and I got the chance to play at Manchester United's stadium, Old Trafford, at half-time. I was buzzing with excitement. It felt amazing to be playing football on the same pitch that my heroes Cristiano Ronaldo and David Beckham had played on. I even kept a piece of turf from the sole of my football boots as a souvenir!

Eventually, that piece of grass withered away and died, but my dream to become a professional footballer and play again on that pitch never went away.

" THAT SEED OF A DREAM GREW. BUT ONLY BECAUSE I WATERED IT. "

Dreams live in our heads. And, unless you do something to nurture them, they can end up staying there. We want to help you water your dream-seeds and let them blossom.

WHAT'S YOUR GOAL?

In this chapter we'll help you to plan a route towards achieving your dream. But you can't plan a route until you know where you want to go, can you? We've talked a lot about identifying your superpowers (what you do well), your spark (what you love doing) and your WHY (the reason you do it). All of these things are important steps towards setting your goals and achieving your dreams. Have a think back to your answers, and now ask yourself these three important questions:

1. What do I want to accomplish?

2. If I was totally guaranteed to succeed, what would I choose to do?

3. If I knew I would fail, what would I still do anyway, just because I enjoy it so much?

These three questions will help you choose a goal while thinking about both the DESTINATION *and* the JOURNEY. That's massively important because of something called 'hedonic adaptation', which basically means getting used to a good feeling.

You know how when you get something new, like a new book, game, trainers or a bike, you feel a buzz of excitement? But then the novelty wears off as you get used to your new item? Well, the same can be true when you accomplish something. Imagine you're playing a game of football and you score a goal. After that initial rush of pride and happiness, after a while you return to how you felt before you scored. This is how humans have learned to adapt to life's ups and downs. So, after any good or bad feeling, we tend to return to the same level of happiness that we had before the good thing or bad thing happened.

This has even been found to happen to lottery winners! After winning millions of pounds, they also eventually return to how they felt before their win. That's mad, isn't it?

This is 'hedonic adaptation'. It's also sometimes known as 'the hedonic treadmill', because when the novelty wears off, it can leave you feeling like you want to keep running after more and more. So, it might make you buy something else or strive to reach another goal, but even after getting that new thing or achieving that next goal, before long you're back where you started in terms of how satisfied you feel.

Now, just to be very clear, this doesn't mean that there's no point going after your goals (goals are a very good thing to have). And this is definitely not me saying, 'Let's all give up – what's the point anyway, if I'll just feel the same afterwards?!'

Instead, I want to make sure that your happiness isn't RELYING on you achieving your goal. I don't want you thinking, 'I'll be happy when I achieve this' or 'I'll be satisfied when I get that'. Because if, for some reason, you don't achieve your goals, you could feel pretty gutted.

That's why it's important to enjoy the journey and not just concentrate on the destination – so you can feel happy now, not just when you get or accomplish something new. And it's also important not to focus all your time on trying to achieve your goals, at the expense of doing other things that will make you feel happy (like spending time with family, friends and pets, reading, enjoying nature, adventures, and all the other stuff that boosts those happy hormones – see chapter three!).

For me, I still have loads more I want to achieve, and I will continue striving towards those goals. But I want to make sure I savour the journey too.

IF YOU PUT OFF FEELING HAPPY UNTIL YOU ARRIVE AT YOUR DESTINATION, AND YOU PIN ALL YOUR HOPES ON TO ONE DREAM, YOU'LL MISS OUT ON ALL THE ENJOYMENT YOU COULD HAVE FELT ALONG THE WAY!

THE THEATRE OF DREAMS

Old Trafford was nicknamed the 'Theatre of Dreams' in 1987 by Manchester United legend Sir Bobby Charlton. My personal dream finally came true in 2021, when I got to play there as a professional footballer, wearing the Manchester United shirt. That meant EVERYTHING to me. It felt like coming home because I'd grown up being a United fan, and so the stadium is a massive part of who I am.

But it's not just achieving BIG-STADIUM-SIZED GOALS that makes us feel good. Accomplishing smaller goals can be just as rewarding.

There's a scientific reason for this! Working towards goals is good for us because it uses the front bit of our brain (the pre-frontal cortex), which is the 'thinking' part. This calms the 'emotional' part (the limbic system), which ends up reducing feelings of worry and anxiety.

Working towards goals is also good for us because accomplishment is one of those pillars of wellbeing we mentioned at the beginning of this book. A dream or a goal gives us something to aim towards, and every time you accomplish something, you:

★ grow and improve;

★ release feel-good chemicals, such as dopamine, in your brain;

★ boost your self-belief and confidence, by proving what you're capable of and showing yourself what your strengths are;

★ build your sense of hope about what's possible.

Ultimately, when you achieve a target, you prove that

YES, YOU CAN DO IT!

As I'm writing this, I'm massively grateful to have played at Old Trafford five times now. March 2022 was the first time we played to a crowd there. It was an unbelievable and unforgettable experience! It felt like the seed of my dream had properly bloomed. Huge posters of each of us lined the concourse and the crowd was filled with family, friends and our amazing fans – the 'Barmy Army' – cheering us on. It felt like such a massive occasion as we walked out on to the pitch. It was a real dream come true.

And my next goal? To score at Old Trafford at the Stretford end (the part where the home fans sit). That's a dream that I want to make happen. And I believe I will one day.

HOPE AND BELIEF: SEEING IS BELIEVING

When I first dreamed of playing at Old Trafford, there wasn't even a women's team at Manchester United! So my goal might have seemed unachievable then. But I was dreaming big. All I knew was that I loved football and I wanted to get as far as I could.

Our thoughts can be very powerful. Thinking you can do something is empowering, while thinking that you can't do something is limiting. If you went into a test at school thinking you're going to do badly, you'd be more likely to get a low mark than if you went into it thinking, 'All I can do is my best, and that is enough.' Or if you turned up at a school concert thinking you're going to mess up your part, you'd be more likely to stumble than if you went into it reminding yourself of all the practice you've done and believing you can do it. Just like if I went into a game of football thinking I've got no chance of winning, we'd be more likely to lose than if I went in believing that we could win.

Researchers have found that our brains function better when we're hopeful and optimistic. This is why being more positive about your chances of achieving your goals means you are more likely to achieve them.

There's this one study, for example, that looked into the effects of being hopeful. Researchers compared groups of hopeful people with groups of less hopeful people, in schools, sport, politics and the military. The groups in the study all had the same level of ability, but the research found that the hopeful people tended to perform better and achieve more than the less hopeful people. That's mad, isn't it?

Hope drives us to succeed – it makes our brains more open to taking risks, solving problems and seizing opportunities. So, when you believe in the possibility of something, you are more likely to TRY, to accept challenges, deal with difficulties and learn from mistakes.

If I didn't have hope and belief when I play football, I'd think it was hopeless to try. I probably wouldn't bother attempting some of the riskier moves I make, and I definitely wouldn't be the footballer I am today.

❝ DREAM, BELIEVE, ACHIEVE! ❞

There are lots of ways you can build hope and belief, and water the seed of your dream. You can:

★ draw it

★ write it

★ or visualize it!

DRAW IT

I was really into drawing when I was little. I used to sit at the dining-room table and draw all my favourite players. I also used to draw my dreams. I drew myself playing for United at Old Trafford and playing for England.

Say you dream of becoming a vet one day and maybe even having your own veterinary practice, you could draw yourself surrounded by pets and pet owners as you stand by the front door. Or maybe you'd love to be a fashion designer? As well as drawing your designs on the page, you could draw a catwalk with a banner that says your name on it.

And don't forget those smaller goals too, like doing well in a science project, winning a race or performing confidently on stage. You could draw yourself in the school science lab proudly wearing a gold star on your top, or draw yourself finishing that race, or smiling on stage as a crowd stands and claps.

WRITE IT

There are all kinds of other ways you can put pen to paper and water those seeds of your dream.

1.	Write a 'self-contract', where you write down what your goal is, then sign and date it. For example:

	My goal: score or assist five goals by the end of this month – Ella, 1st March

	Then you can refer back to this contract to check in on your progress, and keep yourself focused on your goal.

2.	Write affirmations. These are statements written in the past or present tense, as if you have already achieved something or are achieving it now. They can relate to a specific goal or be more general. For example, young me might have written: 'I am a professional footballer and I've played at Old Trafford' or 'I can do whatever I put my mind to'.

Now it could be 'I've scored at Old Trafford' and 'I am confident and at the top of my game'. Write your affirmations down. For example, 'I performed well in the show', 'I am improving my skills with practice', 'I am kind and helpful'. Read them (in your head or out loud) regularly – I would recommend a few times a day – maybe while you're brushing your teeth in the morning and before bed, and before or after each meal. Research has shown that repeating affirmations builds our belief about those statements. Aren't our brains amazing?!

3. Write a letter to your future self from your present self. Write about your hopes and dreams for the future, and then pop it in an envelope addressed to yourself to open in a few years' time. Put it somewhere safe and open it when you're older. It'll be mad to see how far you've come, how you've grown and what has changed.

VISUALIZE IT

Before games, I practise something called visualization. This is where you picture yourself doing what you want to achieve. So I go through all the motions in my head, visualizing every detail and step that could lead to me scoring a goal.

Visualization is about using your imagination to show your brain what's possible. When you imagine yourself achieving something, your mind can't tell the difference between what's actually happening and what you're imagining. This tricks your mind into thinking you've really done something and helps build the belief that your dream is more possible!

1. Practise using the power of your imagination. Picture something you aspire to do and imagine yourself working towards it. Perhaps you want to grow up to be an author? If so, you could picture yourself sitting at home and writing a book. Then you could imagine receiving a call from a publisher saying they want to sell your book. Then, visualize walking into a bookshop and seeing it on the shelves! Try to imagine your dream in loads of detail – where are you at each stage? What can you see and hear? Who are you with? Who's

congratulating you? Feel the tingle of excitement and gratitude in your body as you visualize your dream coming true.

2. Create a vision board. Get a big piece of paper and stick inspirational images and words to it. Print them out, cut them out of magazines (as long as the person reading it has finished with it first!) – you can even add your own drawings. My vision board would include photos of me scoring goals, pictures of the biggest stadiums in the world, medals, trophies, a picture of my pet and also a front door and a house key to illustrate owning my own home. I'd also add inspiring words and phrases like 'yes, you can' and 'Tooney scores' or 'Tooney wins'. What will you put on your vision board? Pin your finished board somewhere you can look at it regularly.

Exercises like these that focus on visualizing good things happening in your future have not only been found to help people achieve their goals, they have also been found to improve happiness, hopefulness and general wellbeing too. Sounds well good to me!

MOTIVATION AND REWARD

Visualizing your dream coming true (before it actually has) is a great way to harness your brainpower to build hope and belief. But it's also a good idea to celebrate each time you actually do accomplish something. You don't have to wait until you've achieved your ultimate goal, you can reward yourself along the way: after completing a training session or when you master a particular skill, or when you make the choice to do something productive like go for a run or practise your instrument instead of watching TV. Little rewards for little wins can keep you motivated (and you can use the TV-watching to reward yourself AFTER you've practised).

My dad used to say that he'd give me £10 for every goal I scored. But then I went and scored ten goals! So that was expensive . . . but rewards don't have to cost money. When you achieve something, you could:

★ treat yourself to your favourite snack;

★ reward yourself with some downtime, like TV or something that doesn't require much effort;

★ share your win with someone you know will celebrate with you.

A good reward is anything that helps you stay motivated and hopeful; something that cheers you on along the way so you can keep going in the direction of your dreams.

GEORGIA

CREATING A MAP TOWARDS YOUR DESTINATION

As a young girl, just like Tooney and Keets, my big goal was obviously to become a professional footballer, and to become the top goal scorer at my club.

Growing up, I always used to ask my mum to go in goal to help me practise shooting. She hated it, but knew it would help me improve, so always agreed to it . . . sorry, Mum! Putting my mum in the net paid off, because with all that practice I ended up achieving my goal-scoring dream. I became the top goal scorer at Blackburn, and then became the top goal scorer at the senior league when I was just sixteen.

> THIS PROVED TO ME THAT EVERY ACTION HAS A REACTION: THAT WHEN YOU PUT IN EFFORT, YOU GET RESULTS.

You don't have to put in practice and effort for hours and hours. It doesn't need to feel overwhelming. But if you put in maximum effort for even five to ten minutes, and practise one action consistently, you're going to get better at it. It's this consistency that is key.

Think of your dream as a destination on a map. If you take consistent action by taking a step forward towards your goal every single day, you move in the right direction towards your dream and will ultimately reach your destination. But if you stand still and just expect you'll end up there one day, you're unlikely to ever make it. The small steps you take will get you from where you are now to where you hope to be in the future.

Action and effort are what turn the dreams in your mind into reality.

CREATING YOUR ACTION PLAN

It's time to plot the route you want to take towards your destination. I like planning. It makes me feel prepared. And it's much easier to stay on track to your dream destination if you know exactly how you're going to get there.

When you play in an attacking position in football, you have to make decisions about what to do next to help you score a goal. You have to decide how fast to run, when to change direction, whether to go for power or placement when you kick the ball. It's the same with any goal off the pitch too: you need to know what steps to take to help you reach your destination and achieve your dream – especially when those dreams are BIG.

South African bishop Desmond Tutu once said that 'there is only one way to eat an elephant: one bite at a time' – not that you'd ever want to eat an elephant! But the point he was making is, when something seems big or overwhelming, it's less daunting to tackle your goal with lots of tiny steps, little by little, rather than trying to race straight to your destination in one go. Just like how you can run a marathon by putting one foot in front of the other, one small step at a time. And doing something is always better than doing nothing. Running for one minute is better than running for no minutes. Doing keepy-uppys for twenty seconds is better than not doing any. And when you start small, you can build up from there. You give yourself something to work from as you gradually increase, step by step, minute by minute, keepy-uppy by keepy-uppy . . . You get the picture!

KICK OFF YOUR ACTION PLAN!

1. Get specific with your goal. A game of football is played across ninety minutes and the season lasts for eight to nine months. But what's your timeline? Setting specific numbers and a timeframe helps make your targets feel achievable. You can then match them or improve on them later. So rather than 'my goal is . . . to score more goals', you could say 'my goal is . . . to become the top goal scorer for my team by the end of the season' or 'my goal is . . . to score twelve goals this season' or 'to score a hat-trick in my next match'.

2. Plot out each action like stepping stones towards your destination. Whether your goal is to pass your guitar exam, give a talk in a school assembly or become the top scorer for your team, think about each action and the order you'd need to do each action in. You could see these individual actions as 'passes' of the ball up the pitch, from kick-off to your goal being scored.

For example:

PASS 1 WATCH: Watch experts on YouTube, whether that's a guitar expert, public-speaking expert or your favourite striker. Analyse how they do it, and learn from them.

PASS 2 PRACTISE: Spend twenty minutes every day after school practising your guitar chords or reading your speech or doing keepy-uppys and shooting at a goal. (Reward: watch your favourite TV show to give yourself some well-deserved downtime and keep you motivated.)

PASS 3 LEARN: Attend your guitar lesson or practise your speech in front of the mirror, analysing and correcting mistakes, or go to football training. (Reward: ice cream.)

PASS 4 GATHER FEEDBACK: Ask someone like a parent, teacher or friend to watch you and help you decide what to focus on next. It might be that you need to work on a certain guitar chord, slow down when you give your speech, or pass the ball faster. Feedback is valuable, so don't take offence if someone tells you what you need to do to get better.

PASS 5 FOCUS: Do an extra ten minutes working on improving those areas. (Reward: hang out with your family or friends, without thinking about your goal.)

PASS 6 GIVE IT YOUR BEST SHOT: Take the guitar exam, or give the speech in assembly, or play the match (and remember to give yourself a well-earned reward at the end!).

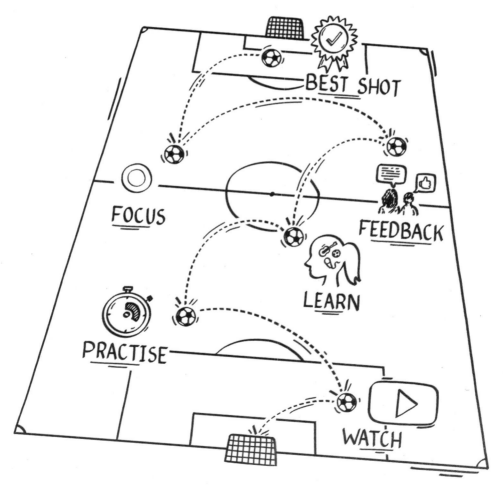

There's something really satisfying about ticking actions off on a to-do list as you go along. It shows you are making progress!

Plus, when you write your goals down with timeframes and you schedule them into your week, it's easier to make the decision to take that action even if you get distracted, because it's right there in your action plan.

Take my current goal to learn German, for instance. I'm often invited to go out for food instead of going to my German lesson, but I know I need to put in a lot of hours to learn the language, so my action to 'Go to German lessons every week' is in my action plan. Scheduling it in makes it easier for me to commit to it and make the right choices, so I can achieve my goal of learning to speak German by the end of the year.

You could also share your goals with other people. We're more likely to achieve our goals when we have someone who can hold us accountable. I tell my mentor and the staff here what my goals are so they can remind me to do my actions. Who could you ask to hold you accountable for your targets and goals? A parent? A sibling? A friend? A teacher or tutor?

Do you know what the best thing about having an action plan is? It's having control over what happens next – like having the ball at your feet as a footballer. YOU decide what passes you are going to make to score that goal. YOU choose whether to pass long, short, do a nifty back-heel or have a shot. It's up to YOU.

It's the same for you when you plan and take action, it gives you ownership over your dreams. And there's a great 'winning' feeling when you accomplish something you've worked towards yourself.

GEORGIA'S GREAT GUIDE TO GOING AFTER YOUR GOALS

Step 1: Identify your destination – the goal you want to work towards.

Step 2: Build hope in the way that works best for you (such as visualization or affirmations).

Step 3: Make a plan, like a map towards your destination – come up with small, specific steps that will help you get there and achieve your goal. Be specific and set timeframes.

Step 4: Put in the effort and practise when you can (even if it's just five minutes a day!).

Step 5: Share your goals – ask a friend or relative to check in on you and motivate you to not give up.

Step 6: Revisit your 'WHY' to remind yourself of the reason you want to accomplish something.

Step 7: Celebrate wins along the way with little rewards.

Step 8: Enjoy the journey! Remember, Plan A doesn't always work out and sometimes life gets in the way. But if you enjoy the process, then you'll hopefully be happy either way!

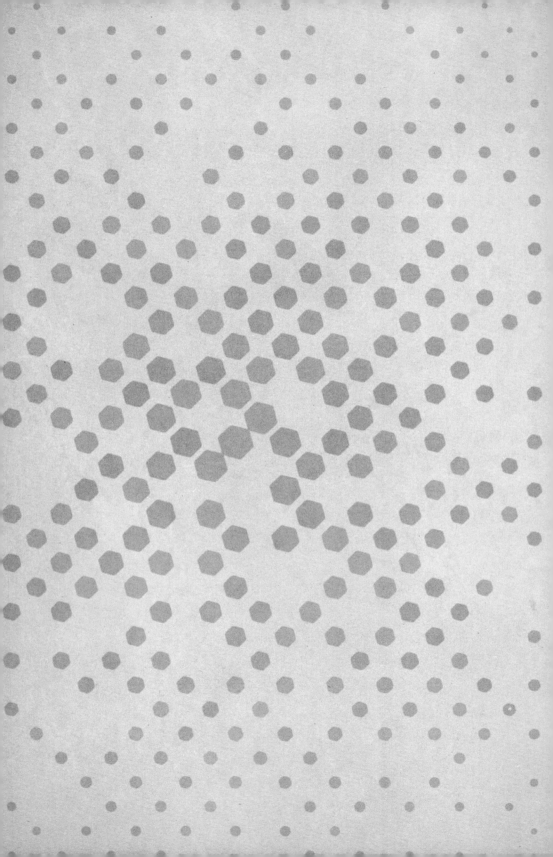

PART FOUR
SHE GOES AGAIN

CHAPTER EIGHT: BOUNCE BACK AND RISE TO CHALLENGES

NIKITA

GO AROUND OBSTACLES

By the time I was ten years old, everything I did revolved around football. Four years before, my next-door neighbour Calvin had knocked on my door and asked, 'Are you coming out to play footie?' There wasn't much opportunity for girls to play football at my primary school so, from the moment Calvin invited me, I played with the boys instead. I loved having kickabouts with the boys in the playground and after school at the local sports court. At age seven, I joined the boys' team, Kingsley United. I was the only girl, but I felt respected, challenged and valued there.

I've always loved watching football too. Growing up I'd watch *Match of the Day* every Saturday, and nobody was allowed to touch the TV while it was on. I enjoyed the commentary and listening to the pundits' analysis of the matches and the footballers. It helped me learn about the different ways that football is played, which helped me learn as a player myself.

I'd marvel at Thierry Henry on the TV as he sprinted down the left wing and curled the ball into the far corner. And once a year, Mum would call me in from playing football on the street fifteen minutes before the Women's FA Cup final aired. That was the only female football shown on TV at the time, so I would never miss it.

'It's about to start, Nikita!' my mum would shout, and I'd race in. It was my television highlight of the year. Partly because it was the only time I could see women playing football on mainstream television, and partly because it was the only opportunity I had to watch my heroine, Julie Fleeting, play.

Julie Fleeting is a Scottish ex-professional football player who captained Scotland, played for Arsenal for nine years and was the first Scot to play professional football in America. She won seventeen major trophies, had 121 caps for Scotland (that's A LOT!) and holds the national record of 116 goals scored for her country. She was and still is a footballing legend, and she was everything I wanted to feel as a footballer.

In 2004, Julie scored a hat-trick, which led Arsenal to FA Cup final victory over Charlton.

But the year after, at the start of the new season, a curveball was thrown my way. The Kingsley United coach pulled me into another room just before the first league game. He explained that under current FA rules, from the age of twelve, I would no longer be allowed to play league matches alongside boys. Mixed teams were for under elevens only, so now that I was eleven, this would be my last season with Kingsley United.

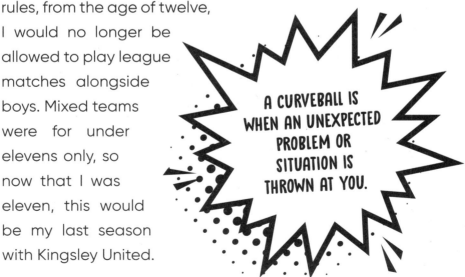

A CURVEBALL IS WHEN AN UNEXPECTED PROBLEM OR SITUATION IS THROWN AT YOU.

I was devastated. And determined! Stop playing football in my local community? Me? No way!

In fact, a year or so before finding out that this would be my last season with the boys' team, something else had happened that could have meant leaving Kingsley United – although, rather than an obstacle, this had been an opportunity.

When I was ten, a woman had approached my mum while she stood watching me play for my team. She introduced herself as Mo Marley, the head coach at Everton Ladies.

'YOUR DAUGHTER'S GOT TALENT', SAID MO.

She was interested in me playing for Everton. But when my mum told me, I said, 'No, I'm not leaving Kingsley.' I wasn't ready for that opportunity. I loved my team too much to leave. For me, Toxteth was my sanctuary and Kingsley United my extended family. And what the area lacked in funding and opportunities, it made up for in love and support. The multicultural community made everyone feel welcome and I felt at home here.

But eighteen months later I didn't have a choice. I was no longer allowed to play with the boys' team.

I still didn't want to go to Everton though, and I didn't want to go and find a girls' team outside my community either. I didn't want to travel for football, I just wanted to stay where I was, playing with friends and family members in a community-based team with a community feel. I wanted to stay playing for Kingsley United. So I went to see Earl, the founder of Kingsley United, to see what could be done.

Earl told me how there was already a girls' league, so we would need to get the team together by the spring in order to register in time for pre-season training. So, for the next six months, during my last season with the boys, I went around all the local youth clubs asking girls if they wanted to form a new girls' football team with me. I asked girls in my family, girls at school, girls in the neighbourhood, any girl I saw kicking a ball – even any

> AS SOON AS WE STARTED TALKING, I KNEW EXACTLY WHAT I NEEDED TO DO. I WAS GOING TO FORM A GIRLS' TEAM RIGHT HERE IN THIS COMMUNITY, MY COMMUNITY – KINGSLEY UNITED GIRLS!

girl I passed in the street! Over the summer holidays, Earl helped find and organize coaches, sort the training sessions, and check the availability of pitches ahead of the new season.

Each time a girl agreed to join the team, they were invited to pre-season training on the local Astro pitch three times a week from five until seven o'clock. There was a lot of organization but, in the end, it all came together.

That September, we started with fifteen players, although at one point, half the team were my cousins – two defenders, a couple in midfield, one up front with me and one in goal! Thankfully, at least twelve of us turned up every week for the matches, and we went on to become a strong (and very competitive) team. We even managed to win the league, twice!

' THIS EXPERIENCE TAUGHT ME THAT WHEN OBSTACLES BLOCK YOUR PATH, THERE'S OFTEN A WAY AROUND THEM. '

I also learned the importance of staying true to yourself in the face of curveballs. I wasn't about to let the FA rule stop me playing. Football was my spark. Especially playing with my local community. I couldn't let anything put that fire out! So I did what felt right for me. I found my own way forward that meant I could carry on doing what I loved most. And it was those first matches with the Kingsley Girls' team that sowed the seeds for what was to come.

Mo Marley returned a few years later and invited me for a trial at Everton's Centre of Excellence, the club's academy programme for young girls. When opportunity knocked the first time for me, it hadn't felt right to leave Kingsley United. But two seasons in, with two wins under our belt, I felt ready for a fresh challenge, so I jumped at the chance to join Everton.

From taking those first steps playing football with my brothers and friends to joining a team and forming a new one, I'd found a different route to get me where I wanted to be, and when an obstacle threatened to get in the way, I'd headed that curveball away.

OPT FOR **OPTIONS**

Sometimes, a curveball can feel devastating, like it's the END OF THE WORLD. But, even if Plan A (for me, continuing to play with the boys' team) is no longer possible, you still have options that will help you keep going one way or another. (Tooney will share more about her experience of this on page 324.)

In football practice, if you miss the target, you try again and again and again. You keep trying to score and if it doesn't work, you change what you're doing; you find another way. The same is true if you make a mistake in music practice – you keep playing the instrument until you nail the tune. In fact, whenever you're faced with an obstacle in your path, you don't need to stop and give up, you just need to find a way around it.

For me, when that curveball from the FA got in my way, I had some options:

★ I could write to the FA and relentlessly demand change for girls to be able to play with boys after the age of eleven. (We thought about taking this option, but I knew it would take a long time. The good news is, as female football grew, some people did speak up about changing this rule, and five years later, in 2011, the FA raised the age limit for mixed teams to thirteen and later to sixteen. Today, boys and girls can play football in the same teams up to the age of eighteen.)

★ I could try a different route or strategy, set up a girls' team or find one that already existed for me to join.

★ I could move away from my family and friends and go to Everton Ladies, aged ten.

★ I could change direction towards a different goal or destination. Perhaps try a new sport or focus on teaching other people to play football instead?

I considered all these options and chose what felt right for me at the time. But none of these are wrong or bad choices, because they all involve TRYING – showing up and giving it your best shot.

PLAN B

Curveballs do sometimes get in the way – sometimes to test us, sometimes to challenge us, sometimes for no reason other than life being a roller-coaster ride! Because of this, it's wise to think about what a Plan B might look like, at the same time that you're plotting your Plan A route.

Looking into other options opens you up to ALL THE POSSIBILITIES out there. It can get you excited about how there is always more than one pathway to doing something you love.

For example, I did a sports course at college, while I was at Manchester City (the kind I later sponsored other girls to do), which made me realize how many different (and fun) options there are for a career in sport. Even though I was still committed to being a footballer, I completed this course in order to understand all the different career paths that I could have had, or that I could still do in the future. It was hard work to juggle football with further education, but I learned that whatever happens, I could still be involved in sport in some way – maybe not being a player, but being a coach, a manager, a physiotherapist (someone who helps athletes prevent and recover from injuries) or a nutritionist (someone who gives guidance on what food and drink athletes should have), plus so many more options.

It can be difficult switching to Plan B when you've had your heart set on Plan A. But you can still get just as much joy out of a new pathway. If I hadn't become a footballer, I'd probably have become a coach or

IF YOUR PLAN A DOESN'T WORK OUT, FOR WHATEVER REASON, KNOW THAT PLAN B CAN BE JUST AS FULFILLING.

a youth worker, something that would have fulfilled my purpose of making a difference. G would've become a police officer or joined the army or been a sports coach – as long as she was outdoors and active, she'd be happy. And Ella would have become a PE teacher or a football freestyler with her own YouTube channel. Just because one option doesn't work out, it doesn't mean you can't still do what you love some other way.

And you never know. Plan B could end up being the happier destination. You might meet someone you'd never have met had you gone down the Plan A route, or you might have an opportunity presented during Plan B that never would have been an option via Plan A.

So stay open to everything, play with all the possibilities and keep enjoying the journey, no matter which path you choose.

Here's an exercise to get you thinking about all the different pathways YOU could choose.

SAY YOU WANT TO BECOME AN AUTHOR, YOU COULD:

★ write short stories and enter writing competitions;

★ get work experience for a publisher;

★ send stuff you've written to the local newspaper;

★ publish your writing online via your own blog.

IF YOU WANT TO BE A TV PRESENTER, YOU COULD:

★ start your own YouTube channel;

★ send showreels to different production companies;

★ make your own mini-production company with a group of friends.

Now think about other goals that would still be amazing to achieve, and that still fulfil your 'WHY' and give you a sense of purpose. For example, if you dream of being an astronaut but Plan A doesn't work out, you could train to become a pilot or get a job working for a space or aircraft agency. Or if you'd love to become a vet, your Plan B could be to become a dog trainer or a horse-riding teacher or to work on a farm.

Write down your own Plan B options and see how many different possibilities there are to do something you love – one way or another.

Of course, sometimes curveballs can be so big they really shock you and make it difficult to pursue Plan A, Plan B, or anything else for a while. Life can throw painful challenges, disappointments, rejections and setbacks at you, and that's something we've all experienced before. So, we want to show you how, whatever happens, it's always possible to RESPOND, RECOVER and RISE!

NIKITA'S NIFTY NOTES ON DEALING WITH CURVEBALLS

Curveballs are a natural part of life. But they don't need to be a reason to give up!

★ When faced with an obstacle, consider alternative routes around it – see it as a bump in the road, rather than a locked door.

★ Stay open to different possibilities and options. There are so many opportunities out there to do something that you'll enjoy, which use your unique skills and strengths.

★ Be prepared and have a Plan B. Think about alternatives before starting out on Plan A.

★ Do what feels right for you. Move forward on a different path only when you feel ready.

★ Consider what you might need to work on and improve so that you can keep going through whichever door opens for you.

★ There's always more to learn! Read books, watch YouTube videos and speak to people – you never know what other opportunities and possibilities are around the corner.

GEORGIA

When you're playing a game of football, one small mistake can have big consequences. If you lose the ball, the other team can get the ball themselves and score. If you make a poor tackle, you can end up with a yellow or red card. If you lose focus for just a second, it can mean the difference between a win and a loss. And that's why, when mistakes happen, it's normal to feel unsettled. It's no surprise, with so much pressure on your shoulders, that one small error can make your mind whirr, your heart race and your nerves rise.

' BUT IT'S YOUR RESPONSE TO SETBACKS THAT **MATTERS MOST**. HOW YOU **REACT** AND **RECOVER** FROM A MISTAKE CAN BE GAME-CHANGING – ON THE PITCH AND IN **EVERYDAY LIFE** TOO. '

WHAT TO DO NEXT . . .

If I'm on the pitch, and I continue to feel disappointed in myself after making a mistake, it could end up having a negative impact on my performance. It would be easy for me to start having thoughts such as:

★ How could I mess up like that?

★ Now I've made it easy for the other team to score.

★ What if we end up losing because of my mistake?

★ If I've started the game this badly, it's probably a sign that the rest of the game is going to be terrible too.

★ Maybe I'm no good at football and should never play!

Thoughts like these will end up impacting your self-belief and distract you from focusing on giving your best performance for the rest of the game.

Remember earlier in the book, Ella revealed that Sarina took her off at half-time after noticing she was responding to mistakes in a way that could impact her game? Well, I was taught a similar lesson recently too. When we kicked off at Wembley to play Germany in the

Euros final, I had my first touch of the ball and I gave it away. 'It's OK, Georgia,' I said to myself, 'just ease yourself in.' But I was unsettled. My nerves were only soothed by the encouragement of the girls around me. They responded positively by telling me to 'keep going', and they kept passing to me, showing they still believed in me. I recovered by putting that mistake behind me, rising above it and carrying on. Their response reminded me that my response matters too. Not just in football, in front of a massive crowd, but everywhere.

Giving the ball away on your first touch doesn't mean the rest of the game will go badly, or that you don't have any skills, or that you're terrible at what you do. It just means you made a mistake. And it's the same in day-to-day life too. Making a mistake, experiencing a challenge, or saying or doing the wrong thing doesn't mean you're going to have a bad day or a bad life or that you're a bad person. You just need to learn from it and move forward.

> **ONE GAME DOESN'T DEFINE YOU. ONE MISTAKE DOESN'T DEFINE YOU. ONE CHALLENGE DOESN'T DEFINE YOU. HOW YOU RESPOND MATTERS MORE.**

Life isn't always easy. Sometimes things just don't go the way we hoped they would. Sometimes we fall out with good friends. Sometimes we receive sad news about people close to us. Sometimes we don't succeed at something we've worked hard at. But just imagine your life is like a long, winding road. Sometimes the path is smooth and easy to travel along. And sometimes there are big bumps and storms to navigate your way through. Although we often can't control the challenges that come our way, we *can* control what we do next.

RESILIENCE

Resilience is your ability to recover from challenges and climb over obstacles instead of being blocked by them. It's about adapting to setbacks and persisting, so that you can get back up when life (or a player!) knocks you down. It basically means growing and developing despite life's challenges.

Taking charge of the things you can control will have an impact on how well you adapt, bounce back and recover from setbacks.

WHAT YOU CAN'T CONTROL:

★ Other people's opinions

★ Other people's actions

★ Problems and challenges that arise in life

WHAT YOU CAN CONTROL:

★ Your response to problems and challenges

★ The people you lean on

★ How you choose to see the world

★ How you choose to see yourself

You've already seen how Keets responded to a curveball by finding a different pathway to keep doing what she loved. Soon, Ella is going to share how she recovered and rose after rejection. But first, I'm going to explain how I've responded to mistakes, and the impact your mindset can have on your response.

TACKLING TROLLS

In one game, I received a red card and got sent off the pitch, because of a very mistimed tackle where I ended up catching another player with my boot. Thankfully, the other player was OK and able to carry on playing. But I was disappointed to have let my team down, and I took full responsibility for my mistake and apologized then and there.

When I logged in to social media later that day, I received a lot of messages saying cruel, hurtful and hateful things – most of which were very personal and had nothing to do with football.

REMEMBER:
YOU CAN'T CONTROL OTHER PEOPLE'S OPINIONS, WORDS OR ACTIONS! WHAT YOU CAN CONTROL IS YOUR OWN RESPONSE AND YOUR MINDSET.

We're only human and we all make mistakes, but the messages I received felt like a whole new challenge that I'd never had to face before. I started to feel very low, and I even questioned whether I was a good footballer or not.

So, I leaned on my teammates. They were the people who knew me best, and they were the first to tell me that I am talented, I *do* deserve to play professionally, and that we *all* make mistakes. They gave me the confidence to speak out in the hope that it might encourage online bullies to reconsider before posting hurtful comments to others. Slowly, I learned to cut through the noise and shut out the voices who were doing everything they could to bring me down.

This challenging experience reminded me to only listen to voices that actually matter – those who know me and care about me, rather than strangers who are just lashing out and trying to hurt me.

I wish I could tell you that everyone in the world is kind and caring. But unfortunately there are bullies out there who will say nasty things to make themselves feel better. This can happen online or in person. But you can't control their thoughts or their behaviour. What you can control is:

★ **Your response:** take action and don't suffer in silence. Speak to someone you trust.

★ **The people you lean on:** tell friends, family or the people who care about you how you're feeling. They'll remind you just how special you are.

★ **How you choose to see the world:** try and keep a positive mindset. Remember there are kind people out there, even if you are dealing with someone being nasty right now.

★ **How you choose to see yourself:** remember how great and unique you are – don't let anyone's mean comments let you forget that!

Focusing on the things you can control will help you grow your resilience, bounce back and prevent other people from bringing you down! So, with that in mind, let's pack some resilience tools in that kitbag of yours.

BOUNCE-**BACK**-ABILITY

Here's an experiment to get you thinking about what it means to be resilient:

EGG VS BALL

★ Imagine you're holding a ball in your left hand – it could be a small football, tennis ball or bouncy ball. Really visualize the ball. What colour is it? How heavy is it? What does it feel like in your hand?

★ Then imagine you're holding an egg in your right hand. Again, visualize it. How does it look and feel? How does its weight compare to the ball in your left hand?

★ Now imagine yourself dropping them both.

★ What happens when you drop your ball? And what about your egg?

★ The ball should've landed on the floor and bounced back up towards you. And the egg? It probably splatted against the floor and left an eggy mess . . .

★ The good news is that you are more like the ball than the egg. You *can* bounce back! And when you experience a challenge or a setback in life, picture yourself as that bouncy ball to remind yourself that, just like the ball, you *can* spring back from this.

CHOOSING A HELPFUL RESPONSE

Depending on the challenge or adversity that comes your way, there are loads of different ways that you could respond to it. Say you have cinema tickets for a film that you're really excited to see, but you get stuck in traffic on the way. You can choose how to respond to this inconvenience. You could get stressed and frustrated and angry. Or you could stick the radio on and sing along to the music at the top of your voice!

" TAKING CONTROL OF SOMETHING THAT HAPPENS OUTSIDE OF YOUR CONTROL IS EMPOWERING. "

Your response obviously won't change the situation (you'll still be travelling at a snail's pace down the motorway), as that is out of your control. But taking an action that turns this moment into a more joyful one will allow you to make the most of the situation. Taking the good from the bad isn't about ignoring the hardship, it's just about noticing that it's possible for good things to come from challenging experiences. That mindset – to choose a more useful and helpful response – is resilience.

Can you think of a tough time in your life, and try to remember some good things that came from it? For example, you might think about the lockdown during the Covid-19 pandemic in 2020, as this may have been really hard for you. You couldn't go to school, hang out with friends or do any activities outside of your home. But it might have meant you bonded with your family. Maybe you played board games together or watched films, and this brought you closer together?

Look, I know that when you're in the middle of a difficult or annoying situation, it can be hard to see the good. But guess what? It's absolutely possible to train your brain to become more positive and resilient, and to think more helpful and accurate thoughts. Let's try it out together!

THINKING HELPFUL THOUGHTS

Earlier in this chapter, I gave some examples of negative thoughts I might have when I make a mistake on the pitch. If I were to ask myself, 'Are these thoughts helpful?', the answer would be a firm 'no'.

These unhelpful thoughts are what we call 'limiting beliefs', because they make you believe that you aren't good enough and stop you from reaching your potential. So, in my case, such beliefs about my footballing ability could lead me to stop playing, instead of a more helpful action, such as to practise more.

Another example of a limiting belief could be something like 'I'm not really a creative person'. Some people find art easy, and some people find it difficult. But the danger of stating that you just aren't a 'creative person' is that you will start to believe that you will *never* be creative, no matter how hard you try. That's not helpful or accurate because, even if art doesn't come naturally to you, you can improve with practice. But limiting beliefs will stop you trying to get better.

If you sense that you might be having a negative thought, I want you to put it to trial – to take your thoughts to court! Pretend you're a judge in a courtroom. Put that belief up on the stand and look for evidence. Ask it questions like:

★ Are you making me feel bad about myself?

★ Are you going to discourage me from trying?

★ Will you limit me from reaching my potential?

If the answer is yes to any of these, then it's time to get rid of that thought and think of alternative, more helpful and more accurate thoughts that will serve you better!

For example, you may have recently found some maths homework very difficult so you might think, 'I'm not good enough. I'm terrible at maths.' But when you actually stop and think about it, you might realize that you haven't found *every* maths exercise hard and, actually, you've noticed that some elements of it are starting to feel easier. All of this goes to show that you are better today than when you started, and better at some parts of the subject than others. So, some more accurate and helpful thoughts could be:

★ I'm trying hard to become as good as I can get at maths, and I am improving.

★ With practice, I can get even better at this.

★ Just because I've found one thing hard, doesn't mean I'll continue to find the entire subject hard!

Thoughts like these will encourage you to practise the areas you're struggling with, keep going and never give up.

Training our brains to think more accurately, flexibly and positively is called 'resilient thinking'. This is especially helpful when it comes to facing challenges in life. It's during these tough times that our emotional brains can take over (remember those ball-hogging hormones in chapter three?), and our negativity bias can kick in, causing us to have negative thoughts, assume the worst and judge ourselves too harshly.

WHEN WE PAUSE TO QUESTION OUR THOUGHTS, IT GIVES US THE CHANCE TO TURN THE VOLUME DOWN ON OUR INNER CRITIC, AND TURN THE VOLUME UP ON OUR INNER CHEERLEADER. THIS HELPS US BECOME MORE RESILIENT.

It's time to put this into practice! I'm going to list some common limiting beliefs, and I want you to grab a pen and paper and write down how you could reframe these unhelpful thoughts into something more accurate, flexible and positive. I'll give some examples to start you off:

LIMITING (UNHELPFUL) BELIEF	REFRAMED (HELPFUL) BELIEF
'I'll never be able to draw! I'm not creative enough.'	'Art isn't my strongest skill, but I can have a go, try my best and get better with practice.'
'I'm no good at science. I'm going to fail my test.'	'For my last science test, I put extra effort into revising, as I know this subject is one I sometimes struggle with. I passed the test, and so if I put in more effort again, I have a better chance of passing this next test too.'
'I'm not sporty or fast, so I'll never make the netball team.'	'Running fast isn't a skill of mine yet, but I am quite good at catching, so I could still be a valuable team member. And the more I practise running, the faster I'll become.'

Now it's your turn. Copy out the below table on a piece of paper and fill in the second column.

LIMITING (UNHELPFUL) BELIEF	REFRAMED (HELPFUL) BELIEF
'I don't deserve to win. I'm just not good enough!'	
'I can't stand up and present in front of my class. I'll mess up.'	
'I shouldn't bother trying, in case I get it wrong.'	

Hang on to this list of positive beliefs – you never know when it might come in handy to refer back to!

TRAIN YOUR BRAIN

Have you ever heard the saying 'what doesn't break you makes you stronger'? This is a common – and very true – phrase. But what does it actually mean?

Well, facing a challenge encourages us to flex our resilience muscles. Each time we use them, they become stronger. Just like exercising your body builds your physical muscles and makes them stronger, overcoming setbacks trains your brain to become mentally fitter and overcome other difficulties again in the future. This means EVERYTHING COUNTS towards training your brain to be more resilient – even the hardships and challenges (especially them!).

❝EVERY TIME WE DEAL WITH SOMETHING DIFFICULT, WE GROW.❞

Tricky experiences can also teach us so much about ourselves. When you do something challenging or face something difficult, you grow more than you would if everything was easy, because you learn things you didn't know before and use strengths you didn't know you had.

This kind of attitude involves using that 'challenge mindset' that we spoke about in chapter two – the idea that your confidence grows with the more challenges you overcome and the more you stretch outside of your comfort zone. When you have a challenge mindset, you see challenges as a chance to get through something tough and grow from the experience. Having this mindset means you realize that these situations can test you in a good way by helping train your brain to become mentally fitter and stronger.

EVERY CLOUD HAS A SILVER LINING

There is value in difficulty. For example, loss can teach us to be grateful for what we have, injustice can spur us on to demand positive change, and unexpected change or uncertainty can reveal unexpected possibilities and opportunities.

When my parents split up when I was young, it was completely outside of my control and I couldn't do anything about it. So instead of dwelling on the negative side of how things would be different, I was encouraged to focus on the good that came out of it.

For example, them going their separate ways gave me more quality time with each of them individually. (And I'm not going to complain about getting double presents at Christmas and birthdays!) Plus, later, I ended up with two more brothers on my dad's side, which was fun for me.

Obviously, because there was friction before they split up, not every day was a good day in the family. But this experience gave me a much greater understanding of other people's emotions. Plus, I now think I'm much better at seeing both sides of a situation.

Taking the good from the bad is about noticing that it's possible for good things to come from difficult experiences. This makes it easier to recover and rise from them.

And besides, if life was always easy, you wouldn't appreciate the good stuff as much. Although I obviously love winning matches and tournaments, if we won every single game, I wouldn't appreciate winning as much as I do, and I wouldn't grow and learn from these experiences either. Failure teaches you what not to do next time! So it's useful to get things wrong sometimes. You learn lessons that you wouldn't have had the opportunity to learn otherwise.

WE NEED RAIN TO GET RAINBOWS, WE NEED TO FAIL AND MAKE MISTAKES IN ORDER TO LEARN, AND WE NEED LOSSES TO APPRECIATE THE WINS. THAT'S HOW LIFE WORKS.

The good news is that this means there is no such thing as failure, and for me that's a huge relief! Even when you struggle or get something wrong, you can always gain something valuable from doing it, which means you haven't *really* failed, have you? It's like Nikita says, the only way she'd ever truly fail is if, after missing a penalty, she didn't step back up to that penalty spot again. If she learns from a miss and goes again, she hasn't failed – she's shown resilience.

The most successful people in the world will tell you that they failed several times before they became successful. In fact, many attribute their success to learning from all the things they got wrong on the way to the top.

❛ SO WHAT'S THE HARM IN TRYING, TRYING AND TRYING AGAIN? ❜

THE GOLD IN YOUR MISTAKES

Getting things wrong is a natural part of being human. So, whenever you make a mistake, you have a choice. You can either:

★ beat yourself up about it and end up feeling (and performing) worse, or

★ give yourself permission to be human and resolve to learn from your mistakes so you can do things differently (and better) next time.

Here's a little exercise you can try. Think about a mistake you've made and ask yourself:

★ What happened? What was the mistake?

★ What did I learn from that mistake?

★ What would I say or do differently next time I'm in that situation?

★ How has that mistake had a positive impact?

Here are my own answers to those questions:

WHAT HAPPENED?

In one of the teams I used to play for, I was often called upon to replace injured or resting players – no matter what position they played. This meant that in every game, I was playing in a different position. I could feel that I wasn't improving because I wasn't able to focus on just one position. My mistake was staying silent. I didn't speak up about my concerns, which meant I stopped developing as a player for a while, and almost missed out on playing in the Euros.

WHAT DID I LEARN?

I learned that it's important to speak up for myself and my own needs, instead of worrying about what others might think. You have to let people know if you're not happy, if you're feeling frustrated or if you want something to change.

WHAT COULD I DO DIFFERENTLY NEXT TIME?

Speak up sooner!

HOW HAS MAKING THAT MISTAKE HAD A POSITIVE IMPACT?

Making this mistake at the club was valuable because it gave me the fire I needed to speak up when it mattered most. So, when Sarina was making her selections for the England squad, this lesson came in very useful. During a qualifier for the Euros, I had a conversation with Sarina where she told me that she didn't really know where I fitted in the team and wasn't sure where she wanted to play me. Realizing I might not make the squad if I stayed silent, I finally spoke up.

I believed in myself and knew the qualities I could bring to the team. And I told Sarina that. Then, after using my voice to talk about where I felt I fitted in the team, I let my football do the talking by getting an assist and scoring a penalty!

YOUR TURN!

Think about a recent mistake you've made and ask yourself these questions. Hopefully this will show you how every mistake can be a useful lesson and an opportunity for growth – and no obstacle needs to stop you from going after your goals.

GEORGIA'S GREAT GUIDE TO BOUNCING BACK

★ Focus only on the things you can control.

★ Remember you're a ball, not an egg! You'll bounce back.

★ Lean on the people you trust when you need support.

★ Get rid of those limiting beliefs and look for more helpful, flexible and accurate ones.

★ Develop a challenge mindset and realize the value in tough situations.

★ Remember that there's no such thing as failure.

❝ YOU ARE A LIONESS. YOU ARE STRONGER THAN YOU THINK. ❞

ELLA

RISE AFTER REJECTION

When I was eighteen, after being with the club for two years, Manchester City didn't offer me a professional contract. I was heartbroken. I thought it was the end of the world, and I lost some belief in my abilities as a footballer.

But looking back on it now, it's probably the best thing that could have happened to me. That rejection made me realize that not everything is handed to you on a plate; you have to work hard for it. That determination to work harder has made me into the player I am today. Ever since that moment, every time I've stepped on to the pitch, I've always given 100%.

That knockback motivated me to get my head down and I went into every session trying to prove a point: that I was good enough to sign the professional contract that I'd been dreaming of signing ever since I was a little girl.

The problem was, I still wasn't being given the game time to prove myself on the pitch. I was always on the bench.

'I HAD TO MAKE A DECISION.'

I remember sitting in a coffee shop with my dad and my agent, Gaz, telling them how gutted I was that my dream of breaking into the first team was ending this way. After crying and crying and crying some more, I eventually wiped away my tears and knew what I needed to do.

I loved football too much to be sitting on the bench. I had to find another club that would believe in me.

There were rumours about a women's team being formed at Manchester United. I remember thinking, 'Wow, how perfect would that be for me right now? To play for the club that I grew up supporting and loving?' Fortunately, the rumours were true! And after just one meeting with the manager, Casey Stoney, I signed with Manchester United to join the very first female team for the club.

This journey taught me that when things don't go to plan and when life knocks you down, you have to keep giving it your best shot. There's a good chance something great is right around the corner, even if it might not feel like it at the time. Just never lose hope.

> **" IT'S ONLY BY GETTING KNOCKED DOWN THAT YOU FIND OUT HOW TALL YOU CAN STAND. "**

PERSIST, WHATEVER THE PATH

Imagine you're given a big set of keys to open a games cupboard. You try every single key, one by one, but none of them seems to be able to open the cupboard. Finally, as you put the last key in the lock, the door opens. Life can be like that sometimes. You might try one thing, but that doesn't go to plan, so you try something else, but get the same outcome. The important thing is not to get too discouraged, because, eventually, you'll turn the right key and the door will open.

PERSISTENCE IS A MASSIVE PART OF RESILIENCE – YOU NEED TO KEEP GOING, EVEN WHEN THINGS AREN'T GOING YOUR WAY.

I could have given up that day when City turned me down. And Walt Disney could have given up when his proposal for Disneyland was rejected more than three hundred times before he secured the money he needed to build it!

' GIVING UP TOO EARLY IS WHAT STOPS DREAMS IN THEIR TRACKS. '

And remember that persistence doesn't just mean continuing to do exactly what you're doing. Just like you need to try new keys to unlock the games cupboard, sometimes you might need to adapt, change or switch direction to reach your goal, like Keets did. And sometimes you might need to shift your focus towards a new goal. As long as you aren't giving up, as long as you try different keys in different doors — that is persistence.

We hope the tips in this chapter will help you bounce back and feel strong and resilient in the face of challenges. But we do understand that it isn't always easy. Sometimes, even though you know that mistakes are useful and that challenges help you grow and that struggles strengthen your resilience, getting through tough times can still feel really difficult.

Remember we talked about the importance of savouring and embracing happy moments in chapter one, as they don't last forever? Well, the same applies to unhappy moments – they are just as fleeting. When you're going through a tough time, just know that what you're going through won't last forever, and you *will* come out the other side.

With all the tools and tactics you now have in your kitbag, we hope you'll feel better equipped to face challenges head-on and find your own way through, to keep kicking those curveballs away so you can TRAIN, SHOOT, SCORE and GO AGAIN, with hope in your heart, fire in your belly and a confident, ferocious Lioness roar!

'THIS TOO SHALL PASS' IS A HELPFUL SAYING FOR REMEMBERING THIS, WHENEVER YOU'RE GOING THROUGH SOMETHING DIFFICULT.

EXTRA TIME

We are THREE LIONESSES, but there are millions of other Lionesses all over the world. Not everyone realizes that yet – we *all* need to learn how to embrace the spirit of the Lioness that's already inside us.

We hope this book shows you how to do just that. How to make the most of every minute of your life – by believing in your brilliance, taking care of yourself and finding your spark, so you can do what you love, love what you do and go after your biggest, boldest dreams.

We hope you can make all your minutes and moments count by enjoying the journey today and showing up with effort and persistence to build your best possible tomorrow.

We hope you can pack all the tips and tactics we've shared across these pages into your kitbag, and use them to rise to challenges, step outside of your comfort zone and embrace your inner Lioness, who is brave, courageous, powerful and strong.

A lioness is more than just 'a female lion', just like we are more than just 'female footballers'. We hope you can now go out into the world feeling confident about your unique superpowers and knowing how to respond to curveballs that get kicked your way. Reach up, speak out and keep putting one foot in front of the other as you take small steps in the direction of your dreams.

Lionesses also know there is strength in numbers, and as well as taking care of themselves, they take care of their pride. So find the people who build you up, surround yourself with them, and make sure you're there to support your pride too. Because together we rise.

Passion and resilience are a powerful combination. We hope after reading this book you feel ready to roar, and to go out there and be as fiercely YOU as you can be. So, know yourself and be yourself, rather than whoever the world says you 'should' be.

'THERE'S ONLY ONE YOU AND YOU ARE AMAZING! PLEASE BELIEVE THAT.'

Finally, on the next page are our main Lioness Lessons for you to take away from this book.

★ Spend time doing what lights you up and what matters most to you.

★ Get outdoors and move. Your happy hormones will thank you for it.

★ Be proud of all that you are and all that you have the potential to become.

★ Turn the volume down on your inner critic and up on your inner cheerleader.

★ Celebrate every win, learn from losses and remember there's no such thing as failure.

★ Get to know the unknown and get comfortable with discomfort, so you can reach further and higher.

★ Soak up knowledge like a sponge and practise hard.

★ Focus on what you can control.

★ Be hopeful and kind – to yourself and to others.

★ Lean on those who lift you up, to prepare yourself to rise to challenges.

★ Remember that you can do hard things . . . and how do we know this?

Because YOU ARE A LIONESS!

Thank you for reading our book – it's our very first one and we're so proud of it. You've read about how we got to where we are today. You've seen what has knocked us down and what we've done to get back up. You've read about what we've learned, what we've got right and what we've got wrong. We've shared our stories, Lioness lessons and team tactics.

Now it's YOUR TURN to go out there and write your own story, so we're handing you the pen and we're passing you the ball.

As a fellow Lioness, you are never alone. You've got this and you've got us.

Love,

Georgia, Nikita and Ella

(a.k.a. G, Keets and Tooney) x

USEFUL RESOURCES

DO GOOD

www.dofe.org/thelatest/volunteering-ideas
Find out about volunteering opportunities.
However, check the age restrictions, as many
opportunities are for children aged thirteen and over.

www.nike.com/gb/help/a/recycle-shoes
Donate old football boots and trainers
destined for landfill to Nike Grind
so they can be recycled and reused.

www.kindnessuk.com/acts_of_kindness.php
Kindness UK have lots of acts-of-kindness ideas for
you to try.

FEEL GOOD

www.youngminds.org.uk
Young Minds support young people to have the resilience to overcome life's challenges.

www.childline.org.uk
Childline are there to support you, whatever's on your mind. They offer advice and will help you make decisions that are right for you.

www.childline.org.uk/toolbox/calm-zone
Childline Calm Zone provides breathing exercises, activities, games and videos to help let go of stress.

www.hubofhope.co.uk
Hub of Hope is a database of mental health advice and support.

www.mind.org.uk
MIND is a mental health charity with lots of useful resources.

www.samaritans.org
Whatever you're going through, a Samaritan will go through it with you. Call 116 123 for free, anytime, all year round.

BE GOOD

www.sportsaid.org.uk
SportsAid is a charity that supports talented young athletes to achieve their ambitions in sport and life.

www.englandfootball.com /play/womens-and-girls-football
Get involved in women's and girls' football in England.

www.scottishfa.co.uk/football-development/participation/girls-womens-football
Get involved in women's and girls' football in Scotland.

www.fawtrust.cymru/grassroots/girlsfootball/where-play
Get involved in women's and girls' football in Wales.

www.irishfa.com/irish-fa-foundation/grassroots-and-youth-football/girls-and-womens-football
Get involved in women's and girls' football in Northern Ireland.

www.clubhubuk.co.uk
This kids' activities directory will help you find clubs and activities near you.

ACKNOWLEDGEMENTS

ELLA TOONE

A massive thank you to Gareth, my agent for believing in me from the very start when not many people did. Thank you for caring about me and becoming a part of the family.

Thanks to my family. I wouldn't be where I am without your continued love and support. Thank you all for following me up and down the country and always pushing me to be the best I can be. Everything I do is to make you proud.

Thank you Cheryl for coming up with the idea for this book and helping us share our stories, experiences and tips to help inspire the next generation. Thanks also to Bev James and the Puffin team for believing in this book idea. I've loved being part of it.

And thank you to all those who read this book. Remember we believe in you. We hope our words help you to believe in you too.

GEORGIA STANWAY

A huge thank you to my agents Doron, Hughsey, Luke, Hollie, Suzie, and the team behind the team for the continued support and going above and beyond. Thanks to the team at CAA Base for allowing this to happen; your effort doesn't go amiss.

Thanks to literary agent Bev James Management and the Puffin team for believing in this idea and bringing it to fruition. Thank you Cheryl for your creativity and being understanding, open and honest to hearing my story and helping to tell it.

To my friends both in and out of football, you know who you are. Each one of you will forever be a huge part of my life. To AJ, thank you for pushing me from day one and giving me the platform to be where I am today. And finally, thanks to my family – the Stanways and Cleggs! Your sacrifices made this unbelievable journey possible and seeing you in the stands makes it all worth it! Thank you for pushing and loving me. Let's not stop here.

NIKITA PARRIS

First and foremost, I'd like to thank my family for supporting me through all the ups and downs that sport can bring. Like we say in the book, life and following your dreams can be a real rollercoaster ride and your constant support has helped make the ride smoother for me. Thank you all.

Thanks to my teachers, coaches, team-mates past and present for helping me to become a better player and, most importantly, a better human being. Thank you for helping me to grow.

I'd like to thank my agent Tobi for always having my back. What started off as a player-agent relationship turned into a friend-family bond for life.

Thanks to Cheryl Rickman and Cat Sims, Bev James Management and Puffin for bringing this book together so that we can give the next generation the tools they need to believe in themselves and thrive. For me, inspiring and guiding the next generation has always been important.

And finally, thank you to my sponsors, commercial partners and agencies for all the support you've given. Long may it continue. Thank you all.

CHERYL RICKMAN

A book, like a game of football, takes a team to make it the best it can be. I'd like to thank all those who helped bring the seed of this book idea to fruition. My football-mad daughter, Brooke, for inspiring my interest in women's football; Bev James for responding to the book pitch so promptly and helping us find the right home for *Three Lionesses*; Suzanne, Hollie and Doron at CAA Base; Juliet and Harvey at Be-Engaged; agents Gaz and Tobi. Thank you Puffin team for giving this book a home and for turning it from manuscript to actual book so brilliantly – editors Phoebe, Sarah and Philippa. Designer, Alice and the wonderful Cat Sims for bringing the girls and the words to life with such great illustrations. Thank you to the marketing and PR team, led by Charlotte and Lauren, for helping spread the word about the book. Books have the power to equip and empower their readers, and it's been a pleasure to work on this book with such wonderful people. The biggest thanks of all go to the THREE LIONESSES who made this book possible – the inspirational (and very lovely) GEORGIA, NIKITA and ELLA. Thank you all for giving up your time, sharing your stories and doing all that you do – both on and off the pitch – to inspire the next generation of Lionesses. We'll keep cheering you on, thank you for cheering us on too.